The House of Klein

THE HOUSE OF
Klein

Fashion, Controversy, and a Business Obsession

LISA MARSH

WILEY

John Wiley & Sons, Inc.

Published by John Wiley & Sons, Inc., Hoboken, New Jersey.
Published simultaneously in Canada.

For general information on our other products and services please contact our Customer Care Department within the United States at (800) 762-2974, outside the United States at (317) 572-3993 or fax (317) 572-4002.

Wiley also publishes its books in a variety of electronic formats. Some content that appears in print may not be available in electronic books. For more information about Wiley products, visit our web site at *www.Wiley.com*.

Library of Congress Cataloging-in-Publication Data:

Marsh, Lisa, 1967–
The House of Klein: fashion, controversy, and a business obsession / Lisa Marsh.
p. cm.
Includes bibliographical references and index.
ISBN 0-471-45563-6 (CLOTH)
1. Klein, Calvin, 1942–   2. Fashion designers—United States—Biography.   3. Costume design—United States—History—20th century.   4. Calvin Klein, Inc.   I. Title.
TT505.K58M37   2003
338.7'687'092—dc21

2003010882

Printed in the United States of America

10 9 8 7 6 5 4 3 2 1

Contents

Acknowledgments

Writing a book about a person who doesn't want to be written about is certainly a challenge, particularly when that person is perceived to wield power. I thank those people—current and former employees, licensees, publicists, and industry experts—who took the time to speak to me and share their unique experiences. I am indebted to them.

This process is one that is not possible without copious amounts of assistance. For that, I thank the following:

Eric Simonoff, agent extraordinaire and even better friend

My editor, Matt Holt, for the great idea and support through this first-time process

Mark Ellwood, for your tenacity, insight, and enthusiasm while reading the early drafts

Research assistant Christie Herring and transcriber Ben Winters, for brilliance on a deadline, and also Bruce Furman for getting the research ball rolling

Photo researcher Maria Fernandez, for rising to the challenge in challenging times

The *New York Post,* particularly my former colleagues in the business section for their humor, knowledge, and levity

My former editors at Fairchild Publications, particularly Sid Rutberg, Edward Nardoza, William Taffin, and Jean E. Palmieri for a grueling but useful early education

Christina Care Kearney, Jeane MacIntosh, Sheila Aimette, and my sister, Wendie Marsh, for your friendship and for keeping me sane throughout this process

Dan Mangan, for your love, support, and toenails. This wouldn't have been possible without you

And finally, my parents, Don and Joanne Marsh, for supporting my many forays into uncharted territory without question. This book is dedicated to you.

Prologue

Calvin Klein is a man of contradictions.

This man, who lent his name to a company that has become the brand that is synonymous with American fashion, is its single best ambassador, yet he can be its biggest liability when it comes to dealing with the press and, by an extension, the public.

However, because his is the personality most associated with the $3 billion company, you'd expect him to be just a bit more *tempered,* or perhaps just more in control of what can be a roaring temper.

As a business reporter for the *New York Post* charged with covering the industries of fashion and retail, I dealt with designers of Klein's caliber for years. For the most part, designers and the executives who run their companies are as consistent on a face-to-face basis as they are when put on the spot about bad earnings.

Consider the scene: It is Thursday after Labor Day in 2002. After a long, hot summer, socialites and fashionistas are ready for the fall social season to start, and Calvin Klein is hosting the first A-list event of the season.

The reception/benefit for the American Ballet Theater at Klein's Madison Avenue flagship store attracted just about every fashion-loving socialite in town, along with a gaggle of ballet dancers and celebrities, including Marianne Faithful, Ross Bleckner, and Iman, who joined in on cocktails, canapés, and all-around socializing in support of the ballet.

Calvin seemed to be in a particularly good mood that evening by all accounts, and his visage did not prove otherwise. The tanned designer looked slim and well rested. He was holding court in the front corner of his store, surrounded by courtiers like Paul Wilmot, his longtime publicity consultant, his wife Kelly, and *Interview* magazine's Ingrid Sischy.

Having interviewed and met him several times, I felt comfortable entering his sphere to say hello.

"Calvin, Lisa Marsh, from the *New York Post,*" I said, extending my hand.

He looked at me for a moment and then a flash of recognition came across his face. "Lisa," he said as he wrapped his arm around me and leaned in to give me the fashionable kiss on the cheek. "Of course."

"You know Barry always tells me I should read the *Post*'s business section—that it is the best," he said, referring to his childhood friend and business partner, Calvin Klein CEO Barry Schwartz.

I thanked Calvin, and at that point Wilmot joined our conversation. "Calvin, you know Lisa Marsh, she writes that marvelous fashion business in the *Post,*" Paul said.

"Yes," Calvin said. "You know," he added in a conspiratorial tone as he leaned into me, "you wrote a story about the company that was not quite right. I wonder if I could call you to talk off the record about these things."

I assured him that he could—that I was trustworthy for background information—and Paul Wilmot agreed.

After that quick interaction, I was off, circulating through the party feeling like a million bucks, having experienced the legendary Calvin Klein charm.

Fast-forward two months, to early November. In that time period, I had made the agreement to write this book, the deal had been mentioned in *Women's Wear Daily* (*WWD*), the bible for the fashion industry, and I had been contacted by the Klein people about the book.

I knew it was highly unlikely that Klein would agree to participate in this book, even though it was being positioned and reported as a business biography. Throughout the designer's career, he has been dogged by rumors about his sexuality, illnesses, illicit drug use, and shady business dealings and had already been subjected to an unauthorized biography that splashed the rumors and innuendo for all to see.

In fact, the earlier work, *Obsession: The Lives and Times of Calvin Klein,* by celebrity biographer Steven Gaines and former *Wall Street Journal* reporter Sharon Churcher, almost didn't see the light of day. The duo originally signed a $400,000 deal with G.P. Putnam & Sons to create the book. They reportedly did over 1,000 interviews and spent three years researching and writing. Around the time the book was due to be submitted to its publisher, New York media watchers whispered that someone from Klein's camp—a friend of the designer—had offered Putnam $5 million to quash the book, making it disappear forever. The book, originally scheduled to be published in fall of 1993, was dropped by Putnam for no apparent reason. The authors were allowed to keep their advance and were free to find another publisher for the project.

The authors were eventually able to find another

publisher, Birch Lane Press, which published the book in fall 1994 to much press for the scandalous material it contained.

Not wanting a similar situation to occur and because I was writing a *business* biography, I decided to play offensively and forwarded a synopsis to Paul Wilmot with the understanding he would pass it along to Calvin. My hopes were that he'd see I was writing a completely business-based biography and agree to sit for a series of interviews. Realistically, though, I knew the best I could hope for was access to an official spokesperson, someone sanctioned by Klein to tell his side of the story for background purposes. I had to at least make the attempt.

The designer was hosting another event at his Madison Avenue store in New York, and because my repeated calls to Klein's publicity department were not returned, I intended to put him on the spot and speak to him about my book project.

The event was celebrating an art installation by Italian artist Fabrizio Plessi and attracted the likes of artist Jeff Koons, director Todd Solondz, actors John Cameron Mitchell and Taye Diggs, Eva Amurri (Susan Sarandon's daughter and an actress), and musicians Tricky and K. D. Lang.

Amid this heady scene, which included logs floating from the ceiling of the store (the art), I staked out Klein and made my move to speak to him about his cooperation.

I made my usual introduction, to which he stared stonily at me, offering a begrudging hello instead of the warm embrace I received in September. I plunged right into the topic of his cooperation, to which he matter-of-factly replied, "I'll read your book."

When pressed about sitting for interviews, he looked as though I were asking him to pluck the hairs from his head one by one. "I couldn't do that," he said, elaborating, "I have to design and have more events like this." He said also something about a vacation.

At this point, his coolness was starting to turn hostile. My companion that evening, a particularly tenacious British travel writer, kept quizzing Klein on why he wouldn't sit for interviews, trying to make a logical case while I took a step back to view this scene.

Klein was actually starting to sweat and looked around the room nervously, as though he wanted someone to save him from our "torture." Needless to say, when we stepped away from the designer, there were no social kisses on the cheeks.

Klein was so enraged by our encounter that, while he was a guest at a dinner thrown by Blaine and Robert Trump for the viscount and viscountess Linley later that night, he spent the entire evening spewing venom about me, this book, journalists, and publicists in general for all to hear. In fact, an acquaintance attending the dinner was so put off by Klein's manner that this person has vowed to avoid Calvin Klein—the person and the products—entirely.

These two examples demonstrate that this designer can be the most charming and entertaining person in the room, but can also be the most offensive and invective, not unlike the images the company has put forth over the years. The warmth, playfulness, and familiarity of model Christy Turlington frolicking on a beach with her partner and two children in the Eternity fragrance ads is the polar opposite to the stark cK commercials that appear to re-create a casting call for a porn flick, complete with seedy paneling on the walls and the creepy voice off-camera asking provocative questions. Certainly, it's a company's prerogative to court as many customers as it sees fit, but at what cost to the overall brand image?

Calvin Klein, the company, is also rife with contradictions.

The brand is arguably the most well-known fashion

brand in the world. It would be safe to say that almost every man, woman, and teen in America has owned something that bears the Calvin Klein label at one point or another. To most fashion watchers, professional and pedestrian, the company's brand can be summed up in a few words—modern, clean, sleek, and American.

I came of age with this company. I was a teenager during the designer jeans craze and graduated to Calvin Klein Sport when it was introduced. I fondly remember my stone-colored twill Calvin Klein Sport shirtdress with a wide leather belt, purchased at discount retailer Syms. An adult friend had arranged an appointment with the hottest hairdresser in my suburban town, to which I wore the dress. And for the first time in my life, I was called chic—by a hairdresser, no less. It was one of my seminal fashion moments.

With its far-reaching tentacles, most would make the leap that Calvin Klein, Inc., was a blockbuster business, reaping beaucoup bucks for its owners, Calvin Klein and Barry Schwartz (until the company was sold to Phillips-Van Heusen in early 2003). While the company has made untold millions of dollars, it is almost in spite of the efforts of those running the company.

Calvin Klein, Inc., is a company that has a pure brand image that has continued to be pristine regardless of what was going on behind the scenes with the sometimes ill-planned or ill-executed business operations.

The fashion industry is one of the most vibrant businesses in existence. Runway shows, supermodels, glamorous advertising campaigns, and the promise of new wardrobes every season are heady stuff for those on the outside looking in.

The truth of the matter is very different. For every designer who becomes a household name there are hundreds in the trenches striving for name recognition. It is that very rare harmonic convergence of financial backing, press support, retail interest, imaging, and, of course, the right styles at the right time that allow one designer to rise to the top.

Many in the industry like to believe the fashion business is all about the design, cut, color, and draping of garments—that it is an artistic endeavor—that the fashion industry is one based more on creativity than on commerce.

However, the American designer houses that have reigned supreme—Polo Ralph Lauren, Tommy Hilfiger, Donna Karan, and, of course, Calvin Klein—have proven that design is a small part of the business of fashion. These businesses draw breath from things like the marketing and positioning of the company's image, shrewd partnerships with retailers, regular support from the fashion press, and above all, astute business management who can see beyond the hype.

Calvin Klein is the last great American fashion designer. With sales of an estimated $3 billion annually, few can match his achievements as a fashion designer, as a businessman, and most important, as an image maker.

The story of Calvin Klein is a story that typifies the American dream: Two kids from the Bronx wanted to make money, found a niche, and built a multi-billion-dollar business. While Klein and Schwartz have made some very costly and public mistakes along the way, the key to their success has always been their determination to retain control of the company's most important asset—its image.

CHAPTER 1

From the Bronx

The Mosholu Parkway section of the Bronx was a melting pot of cultures, including immigrants from eastern Europe and Ireland, along with some Italians. "You couldn't avoid intermingling," said Lloyd Ultan, the Bronx borough historian. "There'd be an Irish pub next to a Kosher butcher shop."

The area offered these newly arrived Americans an alternative to living in the crowded conditions of the Lower East Side, another common destination for newcomers. Because of New York's burgeoning public transportation system, living in this distant part of New York City wasn't a bad alternative.

"The subway, up until 1948, was a nickel," Ultan said. "There were no tokens—you'd simply put a nickel into the slot."

It was the living conditions that made the Bronx really appealing. Rents were cheaper for apartments in buildings that were newer—built mostly in the 1920s—and that offered more amenities than the alternatives on the Lower East Side.

The apartments of this area were also more spacious than their Manhattan cousins and came complete with decorative touches of the day—moldings on the walls and wall sconces for electric lights. There was only one bathroom in the apartment, no matter how many bedrooms the apartment had. The kitchen was deluxe, complete with gas stove and a refrigerator, but no icebox. "Nobody had an icebox," Ultan said.

The environment itself was considerably different from supercramped lower Manhattan. "It was, to use the expression of Calvin Klein's parents' generation, 'like country,' " Ultan said. "There were trees, grass, and fresh air all around you . . . the Mosholu Parkway itself is a park."

It was in this environment that Leo Klein, who emigrated from Hungary when he was only 11, and Flore (pronounced "Flora") Stern, the daughter of an Austrian immigrant and an American dentist, met, married, and settled down to raise a family at 3191 Rochambeau Avenue.

Calvin Richard Klein was born into this world in November 1942, the second of what would ultimately be three children.

The world in which the Kleins lived was dominated by hard work. In most cases, both parents in a household held jobs, sometimes laboring six days a week. Leo, who had once owned a grocery in Harlem, eventually went to work for his brother's more successful operation, Ernest Klein & Co., a grocery store that still exists on Sixth Avenue and 56th Street in Manhattan, though it's no longer owned by the Klein family. Flo, a lover of fine things, also worked at a neighborhood grocery, which helped instill an ethic in Klein that would allow him to build his company into a multi-billion-dollar operation.

It was an environment where owning and operating your own business was the way to get ahead. Flo's mother, Molly Stern, was an accomplished seamstress who operated a notions shop and tailoring business that Klein loved visiting as a child. It was said that Stern could make anything from coats to curtains—all without a pattern—a skill her grandson learned from her.

All were striving to make the American dream come true, and if that meant opening a grocery store, selling newspapers, or taking a job working for someone else, that was what was done. Consequently, the children of these strivers couldn't help but be affected by this.

Barry Schwartz came from the same kind of family. Schwartz, along with parents Harry and Eva and older sister Clara, lived a few blocks from the Kleins on Bainbridge Avenue. Harry owned a grocery store on 117th Street in Harlem, called the Sundial, where his mother sometimes worked. Harry and Leo Klein, both grocery owners in Harlem at one point, met while riding the train back and forth from Mosholu Parkway and were responsible for their sons meeting.

Often left to their own devices, Klein and future business partner Schwartz, friends since they were five years old, devised plans for how they could make their own money. It was more about creating a business that would make money in any way, shape, or form and less about the actual method. However, since both the Klein and the Schwartz families owned grocery stores, it appeared that would be the most likely route for the boys, careerwise.

"Calvin and Barry were hell-bent on opening a supermarket, and eventually a chain of them," said childhood friend

Marylyn Aronstein. "The object of the game was to make money. That was Calvin's main objective. It was a serious commitment to being successful. He wanted all the things that we were raised to want."

By the time Klein was old enough to go to school, vast changes were taking place in postwar New York City. Returning soldiers were marrying and creating new demarcations within the middle classes. The creation of and exodus to the suburbs had started, and with it, growth in the economy.

"It was a time of change," historian Ultan said. "Calvin Klein's parents went through the Great Depression and World War II . . . these were the good times."

By the 1950s, the booming postwar economy and the relative affluence it created allowed people in the Mosholu Parkway, the Kleins included, to purchase telephones, room air conditioners, and even televisions.

"These people had more money than they had in their entire lives, or at least in the past 15 years," Ultan explained. "Everybody who lived in the Bronx called themselves middle class."

However, not all was ducky in the Klein household. While others in their community prospered and improved their lots, Leo Klein was simply a salaried employee, much to the dismay of Flo. Years before, Leo was forced to close his own grocery store in Harlem as his physical health became an issue. And Flo's opinion was that his brother Ernest should have taken him on as a partner, not as an employee, or at the very least given him a piece of the business. Consequently, there was never enough money for her tastes, forcing Flo to stretch every penny so that she could get what she wanted, including the fashionable frocks she aspired to wear.

While the Mosholu Parkway was a fine neighborhood, it

stood in the shadow of the Grand Concourse. Inspired by the Champs-Élysées in Paris, the Grand Concourse was the most elegant street in that area of the Bronx, and everything else, including the Mosholu Parkway, was a step down. This was a fact Flo Klein looked in the face weekly, as she made shopping expeditions to stores like Loehmann's, more often than not accompanied by her son Calvin.

"It was very symbolic, especially for Jewish people. If you had an apartment on the Grand Concourse, it was a symbol that you had made it," Ultan said. "The Mosholu Parkway wasn't denigrated, but it didn't have the cachet of the Grand Concourse," something that drove Flo and, eventually, her son.

As a child, Klein took dance lessons at the dance studio that was owned by the mother of actress and director Penny Marshall and her brother, producer Garry Marshall. Dances were held every Friday afternoon at this studio, located above the David Marcus movie theater. "He was a very good dancer," Penny Marshall said. "He wore white bucks and he dressed nice."

The kids of Mosholu played at the Williams Bridge Oval Playground, one of Robert Moses's projects, and perhaps played baseball at "French Charlie's," a ball field named after a defunct French restaurant run by a man named Charles Mangin. However, the most common spot to find the neighborhood kids was across the street from PS 80, sitting on the iron rail fence that ran along the parkway.

"Everyone used to hang out—you'd have a groove on your butt where you used to sit on this fence," Marshall recounted.

Education was very important to the families of this area. A free public education was seen as a ticket to a professional career as a doctor, a lawyer, or an accountant. And PS 80 was a breeding ground for what would later become a group of stellar achievers.

In addition to Penny and Garry Marshall who attended the school in the same era as Klein, designer Ralph Lauren and comedian Robert Klein were students at PS 80, as was Calvin's first wife, Jayne Centre. Future fashionistas Lauren and Klein didn't cross paths, though. (Lauren was four years older and transferred to a Yeshiva school after second grade.)

"The alumni of the school like to call it the 'school the stars fell from,' " Ultan said, pointing out that many other graduates went on to become successful professionals in fields slightly less public than Klein's.

While Klein was a good student who regularly earned As and Bs, he excelled at drawing and art, so much so that he was asked to paint a mural, which people remembered for decades, in the hallway of the fifth floor. This was a hobby his parents encouraged, and by the time he was 12 he had joined the Art Students League, traveling to Manhattan every Saturday to take classes in sketching and drawing.

When it came time to choose a high school, instead of attending DeWitt Clinton High School with Schwartz and the other boys from the neighborhood (it was then a same-sex school), Klein chose to ride the subway into Manhattan every day to attend the High School of Industrial Art. That "made him unusual," Ultan said. "That would have made him unique in the area."

However unique or out of place Klein may have been in Mosholu Parkway, once he arrived at Industrial Art, he blended right in. In fact, he had such an undistinguished career as a fashion illustration major that few classmates even remember him, especially since he chose not to sit for a yearbook picture.

Still, when Klein was back in the neighborhood on weekends, he and Schwartz were again inseparable. They did things like go to the track (Schwartz's passion) or double-date. When these kids went on dates, it was usually to a local theater, the David Marcus or the Bainbridge Theater on 204th Street near Perry Avenue, or if it was a special occasion, Loew's Paradise Theater on the Grand Concourse. A trip to the Paradise for a double feature and then a treat at either the Krum's or Jahn's, the area's reigning ice cream parlors, "was considered *the* date in the Bronx," Ultan said.

After graduating from the High School of Industrial Art, Klein's parents expected him to go to college. For the young future designer, the only option was to attend the Fashion Institute of Technology.

Enthusiastic to get on with it and actually start work that would be meaningful in his quest to become a fashion designer, Klein entered FIT. Once enrolled and attending classes, the designer felt stifled by the trade-oriented classes he was forced to take during his first year at school.

To entertain himself, Klein immersed himself in an education of his own design, studying the few American designers at the time—Claire McCardell was one—who helped him shape his taste for modern, minimalist design in subtle colors.

After a year of what Klein viewed as mundane training, he took a semester off, determined to break into the fashion business any way he could. Though he wanted a position as an illustrator, Klein took a position as copyboy at *Women's Wear Daily* (*WWD*), the trade bible for the fashion industry. The work was decidedly unglamorous, but Klein thought this would give him a foot in the door to becoming a full-fledged member of the fashion industry. Sadly, no one took the time to recognize the talent in this driven young man. Copyboy Klein slipped through the fingers of an inattentive

WWD, just as photographer Steven Meisel and *Vogue* fashion editor Andre Leon Talley would years later.

Klein returned to FIT the next semester, working straight through the next lackluster year to graduate in January 1963. As in high school, Klein again declined to participate in the yearbook, and because of a typo, one of the school's most successful graduates is listed as "Alvin Klein."

CHAPTER 2

Working

As uneventful as were Calvin Klein's years of studying design in high school and at FIT, his first job working as a designer was even more so.

"I earned $55 a week working for a company that made dresses out of a fabric it called 'whipped cream,' " the designer said. "It sold the dresses wholesale for $6.95 and in the stores for $14. When I went into the shop to cut the first samples at eight AM, my boss would be watching *Captain Kangaroo* on television."

Though he was designing, Klein was not remotely happy—he wanted to design clothes that would take him places. After three months, Klein asked his boss for an outrageous raise—$100 a week—and quit on the spot when he was turned down.

The American fashion industry as we know it today is quite a far cry from what it was in the mid-1960s. American women wore clothing—fashion was something that came from the runways of Paris and was worn only by affluent women who would travel to order new wardrobes each season. What we've come to know as sportswear didn't exist. Women dressed up—in suits for day and in gowns or cocktail dresses for evening. Consequently, New York's Seventh Avenue garment district was a very different place from what it is today. The clothing coming from these showrooms and manufacturers was, for the most part, inspired by the fashions issuing forth from the runways of Paris. In many cases, however, the suits, coats, and dresses were direct knockoffs copied by a dexterous sketcher the company sent to Paris.

Most of those whom we'd call *fashion designers* today were referred to as *copyists* or *stylists* in the 1960s, and they worked in the back rooms, toiling for the label of whichever manufacturing company they worked for.

"After World War II was the first time American designers got their names on labels," explained Andrew Volpe, associate chair of the fashion design department at Parsons School of Design. Prior to that time, designers were "unsung heroes, people working behind the scenes in a back room somewhere."

Klein's favorites, Claire McCardell and Norman Norell, were some of the first designers who had companies in their own names. The 1960s saw growth in this area, with designers like Geoffrey Beene, Molly Parnis, Adele Simpson, and Anne Klein arriving on the scene. Even Bill Blass, later referred to as the "dean of American fashion," struggled to get label credit in the 1960s. Though he didn't have his own company at that time, the "Bill Blass for Maurice Rentner" label evolved, with the size of Blass's name growing with his recognition and following until he actually bought the company.

It was this environment that Calvin Klein wanted to crack into and, subsequently, break out of.

The people who were making money in the apparel industry at that time were players. Referred to as *garmentos,* these men were willing to do what they had to—cut corners, undersell friends, steal designs—to make money. The apparel industry was a rough-and-tumble business, and you either played with the big boys or you folded your hand on the first deal.

Dan Millstein was one of the survivors.

Millstein, a gruff, nondescript man, came from a family not unlike Calvin Klein's. He was the son of an Austrian immigrant who arrived in America around the turn of the century.

The elder Millstein "had been a tailor in the Austro-Hungarian Empire, and at one point tailored the emperor's uniforms," said Anne Taylor Davis, a former in-law and fashion industry veteran. The legend goes that "the emperor gave him a butt of his cigar, which was a great thing to get in honor of how beautifully the uniforms were tailored." However, religious persecution and the promise of a better life in America led him to emigrate. Once in the states, the elder Millstein built a small business on New York's Lower East Side. "He was something of an entrepreneurial man," Taylor Davis said.

Like Klein, Dan Millstein was encouraged by his father to get an education, perhaps in accounting or law. However, while attending New York University, Millstein worked part-time for a man who sold coats and, one thing leading to another, quit school to sell coats full-time. After a series of jobs in the apparel business, Millstein started his own manufacturing company in the mid-1920s.

Dan Millstein, Inc., hit its stride during World War II, making civilian and civil service uniforms for the government.

"He made his first big money during World War II. He had allocations for fabric," Taylor Davis said, while most manufacturers couldn't get any because of wartime restrictions. "I assume they were obtained in a somewhat under-the-counter manner. Nonetheless, he had the fabric, and he could make the suits, so he built quite a successful business."

After the war, Millstein was one of the first Americans to travel to Paris, sensing that there would be plenty of deals to be had in the war-scarred city. He worked with Christian Dior and Pierre Cardin, buying pieces he would then import to the United States with great success.

"I was the first one to walk in on Christian Dior. The soldiers were still on the streets in Paris. We had to walk up the four or five flights," Millstein said of the designer's atelier. "There were no elevators."

"He was one of the first of the manufacturers to go over with some friends from Lord & Taylor," Taylor Davis said. "They tipped him off to what toile [a muslin model of a garment used as a guide in the making of haute couture pieces] to buy and so forth and so on, and then he was flying."

By the time Calvin Klein found his way to Dan Millstein's door, the company was focused on manufacturing suits and coats, with a thriving junior women's business on the side. Millstein's was one of the leading firms on Seventh Avenue and, accordingly, received more applications from young designers than most others.

Through determination and his burgeoning charm, Klein worked himself into the firm through one of Millstein's marquee designers, appealing to Faye Wagner, a flame-haired former model. He gained employment as a designer for the company's missy division, designing clothes for women who ranged into the plus sizes.

It was Klein's special skill to be able to sketch a line-for-line copy of a garment after one viewing, and that endeared him to Millstein. At the time, the designers in Paris were setting the trends and, for a price, would allow American manufacturers to send representatives to their shows. For a several-thousand-dollar cover charge and a guarantee they'd buy a couple of garments, American manufacturers were able to get their best sketchers front-and-center to copy the fashions.

While not the ideal situation, Klein recognized it was one he could learn from.

Earning a mere $125 a week, Klein was nonetheless designing women's coats and suits, a step up from $6.95 dresses. Although he thought Millstein was tough, Klein admitted he had taste and an appreciation for well-designed clothes, as long as those clothes appealed to a mass audience.

"I learned a lot, because he threw me into the snake pit," Klein said, doing everything from beginning to end—sketching, choosing fabrics, and fitting the garments.

Soon, Klein was asking for more—more money, more autonomy, more recognition, and more respect. It didn't help that fellow Millstein designer Faye Wagner managed to get her name on the label—Dani Juniors by Faye Wagner—something Klein desperately wanted.

"Calvin wanted to be in the forefront of the change," Taylor Davis said, citing the movement by designers like Bill Blass to have their names on the labels. "Dan thought, why give, and I'm sure he used this word, a *sketcher* anything? He was the one who built the business, financed the business, had the store relationships, got the toiles—what did this kid do?"

Millstein "was an extremely imperious man," she said, adding that he had all the outward trappings of wealth, but was a real ball buster when it came to business.

"The house in Palm Beach . . . the French impressionist (paintings) that he bought for pennies on the dollar when he went to France," she described. He made the effort "to present this civilized veneer, but underneath it was a real rough, tough guy. He was not a bad man, but a man with an extremely different value system."

Klein's dealings with Millstein deteriorated, though his designs were still an asset to the manufacturer, something he acknowledged by periodically backing down from fights with Klein.

Often, Klein would be chastised when he'd show the executive his sketches, with Millstein screaming and actually trying to hit Klein. However, Millstein's behavior was typical for a Seventh Avenue executive. "The fashion world can truly be a jungle," Klein explained, filled with people who are tough, insecure, jealous, and greedy.

The final straw for Klein was seeing the results of his labor, much to his chagrin.

Millstein made a living from "flash-in-the-pan clothes," unlike the classic styles Klein tried to introduce. "Millstein designed gaudy clothes: bright yellow, orange, and lilac suits . . . real hooker clothes!" Luckily, Klein's exposure to the clothes ended once they were shipped. However, his day did come. "One day, I saw a woman walking down the street in the yellow suit with the yellow fox collar and cuffs, a yellow hat, a yellow handbag, and yellow shoes," Klein said, adding that they were all made by Dan Millstein. "I was sick to think that I had been part of making that outfit possible."

Klein had additional motivation to get a better-paying job—he was getting married to Jayne Centre. Though the couple had met in their last year at PS 80, they didn't start dating until they were students at Industrial Art and then FIT. They got married at the Hampshire House Hotel on Central Park South in 1964.

Klein worked his connections to secure a position at a coat manufacturer called Halldon Ltd., which specialized in faux furs. Luring Klein away from Millstein was somewhat of a coup for Halldon owner Louis Schlansky, who consequently treated him with the spoils of war. He had a four-year contract, guaranteed salary increments, paid salary, and a design studio located adjacent to the showroom, so Klein was able to forge relationships with the fashion editors and retail buyers, a move that would establish the groundwork he'd rely on later in his career.

As idyllic as Halldon appeared to be, Klein was still stifled, and he started designing what would end up as his first namesake collection in his spare moments.

The designer worked on his side project nights and weekends. Still, it took him three months to complete his first collection, which consisted of six coats and three dresses.

To finance his side gig, Klein approached his best friend, Barry Schwartz, who had dropped out of college and followed his father's footsteps into the grocery store business.

"When Calvin asked me for the money to open his business, I said, 'Yeah sure.' He was my best friend," Schwartz said.

However, Schwartz surprised Klein with an offer that gave him pause: He offered him half of his father's grocery business. Schwartz had taken over the business in 1964 after his father, Harry, had been murdered in a botched robbery. He had been working at making the Sundial market a moneymaker and thought that he and his childhood friend, working together, could build the Sundial into a chain of supermarkets.

Though tempted, the young designer, who was struggling to support his wife Jayne and his new baby, Marci, chose to follow through on the pattern he had laid to create his own clothing business. Schwartz, a true friend, was supportive of Klein's decision and loaned him $10,000 that was supplemented by smaller loans when necessary, becoming, at Klein's insistence, his silent partner.

"I don't want the money unless we're partners in this," Klein told Schwartz, stressing that Schwartz's money was as important as his talent. "If you're willing to put up the money, then you certainly deserve half the business."

From the get-go, the relationship proved invaluable to Klein. Whenever he needed extra funds for the side project, the designer would call on Schwartz, who would take money straight from the grocery's register to pay the sample tailor in Coney Island and the patternmaker in Long Island he'd contracted to assemble the minicollection.

When the samples were ready, Calvin Klein took the giant step of incorporating his fledgling company. On December 28, 1967, Calvin Klein, Ltd., was officially incorporated, listing the partners as Calvin Klein and Barry Schwartz.

However, the young designer had to get out of his position at Halldon before he could go any further. While negotiating a four-year contract at the onset of his employment seemed prudent at the time, it was now a bit of a sticky wicket to deal with.

The contract made it illegal for Klein to meet with buyers from Bloomingdale's, Macy's, and Lord & Taylor, which gave him little choice but to give notice and hope that Schlansky would be reasonable and let him out of the contract.

However, the Seventh Avenue rumor grapevine got to Schlansky before Klein did.

Several days before Klein planned to quit, Schlansky confronted him and threatened to confiscate his designs. Klein broke down, crying. "This is the only way for me," the designer cried. "I know you're not going to take away my samples, that you won't sue me." Ultimately, Klein had read Schlansky correctly—the manufacturer let Klein out the door without a fight.

The York Hotel, at 488 Seventh Avenue, was a traveling salesman's haven. While it did have two floors of actual hotel rooms, the majority of its rooms were used by garment salesmen as makeshift showrooms during their market weeks. Retail buyers would usually make appointments to visit these so-called showrooms, but would sometimes cruise the floors, poking their heads into rooms to see what new people had to offer.

In March 1968, Calvin Klein, Ltd., took room 613 at the York, directly opposite the elevator doors. Klein's first collection, six coats and three dresses, was displayed in the small, dank room on a pipe rack. Alone in his showroom, Klein worked the phones his first weeks, trying to lure the buyers and fashion writers he'd become acquainted with through his previous jobs to see the fledgling line.

One month later, Martin Luther King Jr. was assassinated, which set off what were, at that time, the largest race riots in history. The burning and looting were centered in Harlem, where Schwartz's Sundial market was located. Schwartz, who had just returned from his honeymoon with new wife Sheryl, was not able to get to the store until two days later, and what he saw was disheartening.

The store's windows were smashed and the store had been looted. It looked like it had been hit by a tornado. Bags of flour had been smashed and food was strewn every-where. It was incomprehensible and more than Schwartz could bear.

"I filled up four shopping bags of what we could salvage, and I threw the keys into the rubble," Schwartz said. "I never went back."

The following Monday morning, Schwartz joined Klein in the little room at the York Hotel.

Business was at first slow—trickling in at a rate that could not possibly support the two young men and their families. Then the elevator door accidentally opened on the sixth floor, giving a man named Don O'Brien, a merchandise manager from Bonwit Teller, a glimpse at Klein's collection.

O'Brien got off the elevator and introduced himself to Klein. After a quick inspection, O'Brien told Klein to bring the collection to Bonwit Teller on Saturday to show the samples to Mildred Custin.

Mildred Custin, an older woman who was always per-fectly coiffed and made up, was the grande dame of the fashion industry. As president of the tony retailer Bonwit Teller, she could make or break a designer with a single order. She was known for finding new talent and using the weight of her store's resources to guarantee their success.

Klein was leaving nothing to chance for his meeting with Custin. Instead of having his samples delivered or putting them in a taxi to go to Bonwit's on 56th Street, Klein wheeled the sample rack himself from 36th Street and Seventh Avenue.

"I didn't want to pile the clothes into a taxi and crease anything," Klein said. "Getting the clothes to Bonwit's was a nightmare, because one of the wheels [on his rolling rack] broke."

The 25-year-old designer was suitably intimidated by Custin, particularly since she didn't smile once while he was showing his coats and dresses. Then she dropped a bomb-shell.

"Mr. Klein, I will pay you $20 more for each of your coats and dresses than you're asking," Custin said. "You could never make them for the prices you're asking and I want them delivered to Bonwit's exactly the way these samples are made.

"And in return for paying you more than you asked, I want exclusivity."

Though Klein was reeling from the magnitude of what Custin had just said, he maintained his composure, and insisted that was not possible. "Other stores are interested and Bonwit's walked in by accident before anyone else saw the clothes. I'll give you anything you want, but I won't give the clothes exclusively."

Custin acquiesced and subsequently wrote a $50,000 order, committing to make Calvin Klein the centerpiece of the Miss Bonwit salon in 1968.

"What impressed me most was the purity of his line and the simplicity of his designs," Custin later recalled.

The size of the order astounded Klein, as he expected the company to do that much business in its first *year,* not its first season.

Schwartz, who was home watching a football game on television, heard of the $50,000 order from an excited Klein on the phone and nonchalantly asked, "What's a Bonwit?"

CHAPTER 3

Early Years and Jeans

The order from Bonwit Teller's Mildred Custin was just the start of an unbelievable ride for the young designer from the Bronx and his childhood friend. As word filtered through the market about Klein's designs, buyers from other major stores visited the little showroom, more often than not leaving orders. Garfinckle's in Washington, D.C., Macy's, and other smaller, regional stores followed suit.

The orders introduced the duo to the cycle so many in the fashion business get caught up in—borrowing money against sales and payments that will not be made for six months or so. Apparel manufacturers work up to a half year in advance of when their clothes will actually hit the stores. The stores buying the clothes don't make payment until anywhere from 30 to 60 days after the goods are received. This cycle puts smaller companies in a precarious position, as they have to lay out the funds to buy fabric and materials and manufacture the clothes long before they'll see a cent for their efforts. Unless the company has a stash of cash, it has to get a line of credit from a bank or a factor, which will treat orders as collateral against later payment.

Klein and Schwartz chose to borrow from a bank, which offered to match Schwartz's funds if he put in an additional $25,000, taking their total to $70,000—enough to produce the Bonwit Teller order.

It was also enough to allow Calvin Klein to move from the York Hotel to a design loft on 37th Street and Ninth Avenue. Still, suppliers, used to dealing with enormous volume for established companies, balked at working with the skinny kid from the Bronx and his tough-talking childhood friend.

Klein approached leading fabric supplier J.P. Stevens, but was turned down. The company couldn't be bothered dealing with the young designer, thinking he couldn't afford their fabrics.

However, once Klein's first collection hit the stores and sold as fast as it could be delivered, the tables had turned, with the Stevens reps calling Klein to do business.

In those early days, staff was short, and Klein and Schwartz both got their hands dirty, doing everything from selling to shipping, regardless of their respective skills.

"At the York Hotel, we both sold," Schwartz said. "I bought the piece goods and figured out the cutting tickets and I shipped it." He added, "I left all the creative to Calvin."

No detail escaped Klein's attention—he would spend up to four days pinning, steaming, shaping, and molding a jacket.

"It was seven days a week in the shop—often 24 hours a day. Barry and I would ship until three in the morning and then sleep on the convertible sofa in the showroom," Klein said, adding, "There isn't any job in the place I haven't done."

For Schwartz, the early years were the best years, "when we struggled so hard to ship every single coat. We'd get phone calls from people who would reorder at full price," something that rarely ever happens.

"Calvin was doing smart, structured coats and suits," recalled Vincent Rebicek, an interior decorator who also runs a small women's store in Scranton, Pennsylvania. In fact, a friend of Rebicek's, Sidney Newman, was a buyer at Macy's, and "gave Calvin some of his first orders." Rebicek ended up buying from Klein as well.

"By Calvin's request, I put a rack of his beautiful suits and coats in my shop," Rebicek said. "He wanted to see what a reaction they would get. My decorating and boutique clients went wild for his concept of structure and fabrics and tailoring.

"Many women who purchased his original items have all held them in their closets," Rebicek added, many years later.

While all of these orders added up, it was the bold move by Bonwit Teller's Mildred Custin that made all the hard work worth the effort. The store's fashion customer was getting younger, and though Bonwit Teller offered an extensive amount of designer clothing on its sixth floor, these clothes were too old and expensive for this growing demographic. Custin was developing more moderately priced collections, to be housed on the store's eighth floor, and Calvin Klein was picked to be its breakout star.

Custin featured Klein's collection in the store's Fifth Avenue windows the week after Labor Day, kicking off the fall selling season. This was a coup for any established designer, but for a fledgling designer, it could change the whole ball game. In the week following the debut in the windows, Custin featured Calvin Klein in its standing advertisement on page 5 in the first section of the Sunday *New*

York Times. After this grand slam, Klein was on the map and on his way to becoming one of the leading fashion designers of the 1970s.

As the saying goes, it's a small world, but nowhere is that more true than in the arenas of apparel manufacture and retail, particularly in the 1970s. Manufacturers, big and small, all went to the same mills for their fabrics. Sample makers, tailors, and patternmakers all traveled in the same circles, so reputation mattered. The same went for retail buyers—if one store made a big commitment similar to the one Mildred Custin made to Calvin Klein, other buyers would take the time to see what the commotion was about. This also was starting to be the case with fashion journalists.

Name designers were continuing to rise in prominence, in part because journalists like the *New York Times*'s Bernadine Morris, the *New York Herald Tribune*'s Eugenia Sheppard, and John Fairchild of *Women's Wear Daily* were paying attention to these new names, giving them ink and introducing them to their readers. It seemed like all it took was attention from the right editors and you were guaranteed success.

Klein recognized the value of press coverage early on and worked his charm to get in with the right editors. He fixed his gaze on two very different, but equally powerful editors who spoke to the different sides of his personality.

Eve Orton, the fur and fabric editor at *Harper's Bazaar,* was a socialite who had fallen upon hard times. Orton, thrice-divorced (most recently from designer John Weitz), was a European-born beauty of a certain age. A regular on the International Best Dressed List, Orton was known for her charm, sophistication, style, and dark red lips. However, needing to support herself for the first time, she went to work as a fashion editor, joining the junior editors from her social class who were working until they found husbands. Orton took Klein under her wing, both socially and professionally, inviting him to travel in her social circles, as she lent her styling talents to his collections.

Baron Nicolas de Gunzburg held a similar position at *Vogue.* Known as Nicky to his friends, de Gunzburg was of Russian nobility—his father had served the last czar. Born in Paris, he emigrated to New York in the 1930s with only a few family heirlooms and his panache. Still, the silver-haired dandy managed to look and dress the part of a European aristocrat, from his pomaded hair to the silver tip of his walking stick.

As one of the few male editors in a female-dominated field, de Gunzburg held a special position and took Klein under his wing, educating him about the finer things. "He was truly the great inspiration of my life from the time we met. . . . He was my mentor, I was his protégé," Klein said.

Klein did what it took to make the business grow, whether that meant visiting the eighth floor of Bonwit Teller on a Sunday afternoon to help women choose the right coat or traveling to do a charity fashion show.

In the late summer of 1970, Klein flew to California with his samples for an appearance on the Dinah Shore show, *Dinah's Place.* On the way back to New York, he stopped in Scranton, Pennsylvania, to do a charity fashion show for his friend Rebicek.

Rebicek recalled, "I was asked to do a UJA fund-raising fashion show luncheon at the Sheraton Hotel," and he asked Klein to come to the event as a special guest. "He arrived and did a great production, even though some of his bags didn't make it."

Klein even made an appearance at Rebicek's store, where his clothes were sold. "We had a champagne reception and everyone turned out to say hello," even though before the luncheon, people were asking, "Who is Calvin?"

The designer went the extra mile for his Scranton customers, staying the night so he could attend a local party in his honor hosted by local socialites Mitchell and Toni Alperin.

Klein "graciously accepted their offer to give the party because Mr. Alperin's mother was a Seventh Avenue model married to Murray Lincoln, who was a well-known Seventh Avenue coat maker that had helped Calvin somewhere along the way," Rebicek said, adding that he almost didn't make the party. "He got a little high on champagne, and other than my mother talking to him about his commitment, he might have let all of the Alperin's guests down."

Because American fashion designers were still a very small fraternity, the elder members of this elite clique did what they could for the young upstarts. Designer Chester Weinberg, a short, compactly built man with thinning black hair, was a boyhood hero of Klein's. Having established himself as a leader on Seventh Avenue, Weinberg shared the wealth, growing to be a fast friend and trusted adviser to Klein, even helping to recruit design assistants for him.

The staff at Calvin Klein was growing with the needs of the business. Physically, they had outgrown the loft space on 37th Street and, in a twist, rented space in 205 West 39th Street, the same building that housed Dan Millstein. The company hired people to help with sales, including Susan Sokol, who was barely out of her teens. Klein hired Charles Suppon as design assistant, on Weinberg's suggestion, but he was still looking for another.

Weinberg had just the ticket—Jeffrey Banks, a gregarious, black designer with a propensity for anything preppy, particularly plaid. As a student at the Pratt Institute, Banks had been working for Ralph Lauren part-time. However, when he transferred to Parsons School of Design, his schedule would not allow him to continue working for Lauren.

"School said you've got to make a choice," Banks said. "I only had a year and a half left, so I really felt like I had to finish school . . . Ralph was very upset."

Several months after he quit, Banks was in class when a professor told him Calvin Klein was on the phone for him.

"I want you to come work for me," Klein said to Banks.

"The reason I'm not working for Ralph is because I have to devote my time to school," Banks explained.

"Well, listen, I want you to come and talk to me anyway," Klein said, and Banks joined him for lunch in the garment district. Though he insisted he didn't have the time to properly commit to a job at Calvin Klein, the designer offered Banks a job anyway.

"I want you to work for me," Klein said, starting his longtime habit of overpaying employees to get what he wanted. "I'll pay you a weekly salary whether you work for me one day a week or five days a week."

When Banks showed up at the Calvin Klein offices he found he was not the only design assistant. In addition to Suppon, Klein had recently hired a bespectacled young gentleman from Texas named Zack Carr.

Carr was one of a rare breed—those who know what they want to be from the get-go. His artistry started with constant sketching as a child and thrived on trivia about movie stars' wardrobes and which fashion designer was featured in which magazine—*Vogue* or *Harper's Bazaar.*

Carr and Banks were cut from the same cloth. "Zack was incredibly talented and had this encyclopedic kind of knowledge of fashion," Banks said, "some of which I shared. We both loved Audrey Hepburn; we were both Scorpios.

Zack's birthday was the fourth of November, mine was the third."

These were heady days for Klein and Schwartz. Each collection they produced was more successful than the last, both critically and financially. The two friends from Mosholu Parkway were pulling in six-figure salaries and were able to support their families better than they'd dreamed possible.

Klein's designs were evolving from the coats and suits that he made his name on to sportswear—simple pieces in luxurious fabrics. But his signature coat, the updated pea coat, always made it into the collection.

"That was his first hit," Banks said. "Calvin's pea coat was his biggest hit. And every season, we had to do a new variation on the pea coat," whether it was a coat season or not.

"The way you knew it was a Calvin Klein pea coat was, the buttons always came off, I guess because women wore them a lot," he surmised.

Besides winning at the cash register, Klein was critically lauded for the first time in 1973, when he won the first of his three Coty American Fashion Critics Awards. He was cited for creating his own modern and clean school of fashion, a first for American fashion.

The Coty Awards, the precursors to the Council of Fashion Designers of America's American Fashion Awards, were considered to be of the caliber of the Academy Awards or the Tonys, complete with a glitzy awards ceremony at Lincoln Center.

In the design studio in those early days, almost anything was appropriate to try, as designer Klein was learning about fabric, the business, and the customer alongside his young colleagues. Experimentation was not looked down on; in fact, it was rewarded.

In those days Klein's favorite color was chocolate brown. It was on everything from the company's press kit folders to the car Klein drove. As a thank-you for hiring him, Banks decided to make Klein a customized chocolate-brown T-shirt.

"I had a friend who lived in Soho, Tommy Gingerella, and he did silk-screening. I took the Calvin Klein logo off of a brown-and-white folder that we used for press kits and printed it on the sleeve," Banks said.

While Calvin told Banks he loved it, he left it on the shelf in his office.

"A couple of weeks after I gave it to him, Barry saw it, and he asked Calvin what it was," Banks said. Klein told him, and Schwartz asked if it was in the line, because he thought it was great.

"No," Klein replied, laughing, "who'd want to wear my name?"

That got Banks thinking about something for the next fashion show.

"We were working 24 hours a day on this show," Banks said. "We had done T-shirts—mints, pale peach, bougainvillea, turquoise, marigold, orange, and lime. The night before the show, I took one of each color of all the T-shirts down to Tommy, and I had him print this thing on them, and I gave them to all the salesgirls to wear as they sat people for the fashion show."

The "thing" turned out to be the Calvin Klein logo, which soon was in hot demand. Buyers "came into the showroom the next day and everybody wanted the T-shirt that said Calvin Klein," Banks said.

This collection, a departure for the designer because of his use of color, garnered Klein another Coty Award for the second year in a row. It was at this presentation that Klein started to recognize the power of using sex to sell.

At the awards show, Klein chose to unveil his fall collection, with a preview of his resort collection, which included an ensemble made of a bikini bottom paired with a cardigan.

"All these models, in cardigans in lime green, orange, turquoise, and bougainvillea, with little matching bikini bottoms, had lots of glycerin on their bodies," Banks said. For effect, "the light would be very intense, so it would look like sun on the beach.

"We told them in the rehearsal to leave a couple of buttons buttoned for Eleanor Lambert," the very proper grande dame of the fashion industry who organized the awards.

"The night of the show we told them to unbutton it. . . . Of course, these bare breasts were flashed, and it brought the house down.

"It's typical of Calvin, wanting to get his sexy way," Banks said, adding "It was a great moment."

"The thing about Calvin is that he has this sixth sense for knowing what people want before they know they want it," Banks said. "I think that's what's so intriguing about Calvin—he has that incredible intuitive sense."

And knowing that if the people couldn't have it, they'd want it even more, Klein and Schwartz embarked on an unusual store-reduction strategy. Instead of growing the business by selling more stores, they cut the number of stores they sold from over 1,000 in 1973, to 500 the following year, with the goal of selling only 300 of the most elite stores by 1976, in turn raising the quality of the fabrics used.

"We used to make samples out of silk crepe de chine; we shipped polyester crepe de chine," Banks said. "All of a sudden he stopped using polyester—he stopped being afraid, and it took the sportswear to the next level of being really loose and really beautiful. It was kind of revolutionary."

It was in this era that Klein and Schwartz discovered the value of licensing the Calvin Klein name to manufacturers in categories beyond sportswear.

While license deals are a dime a dozen these days, they were just starting to be used as revenue streams in the 1970s. The owner of a brand, trademark, or designer name licenses it to a manufacturer of, for example, shoes. The shoe manufacturer then creates a collection of shoes under the name and the licensor, or owner of the name, collects a royalty on the sales of the shoes.

Without start-up costs and enormous financial risks, "it is an efficient and cost-effective way for the designer to expand the empire quickly," said Nicholas DeMarco, who was licensing director for Pierre Cardin for 12 years.

If the name is established, licensors usually collect royalties of between 3 and 8 percent of gross sales on top of an up-front fee.

"The stronger the name, the higher the minimums that are mandated," DeMarco said, which means the licensor is paid on the guaranteed minimum number sold whether the items sell or not.

However, the key to a successful licensed business is keeping it in line with the main collection it accompanies. Retaining control over design and distribution is key to a good deal.

At the urging of Baron de Gunzburg, the first license deal Schwartz and Klein signed was with the furrier Alixandre. The logic was that if Calvin Klein was designing evening-wear, he had to give his customers something to wear on top of the gowns and dresses. The well-designed Alixandre coats were well received by customers—Klein even made his signature pea coat in sable. And deals quickly followed with companies such as Omega for belts, Mespo for umbrellas, and Vogue Butterick for patterns. This growth and diversification took the company from being Calvin Klein, Ltd., to being Calvin Klein Industries. However, the really big license deals were yet to come.

. . .

As well as his business was progressing, his marriage to Jayne had gone in the opposite direction. Whether they had married too young or weren't suited to each other in the first place, the two had grown apart. They divorced in August 1974, and Klein's new single status allowed him to embark on a fresh chapter in his life. Traveling with Baron de Gunzburg, Chester Weinberg, and that crew, Klein became a regular at clubs like Studio 54 and the Flamingo. Klein eventually became a member of the in crowd, considering Steve Rubell, Ian Schrager, Diane von Furstenberg, Bianca Jagger, and Andy Warhol close friends.

Calvin Klein wanted to design menswear. His modern, minimalist designs could easily be interpreted in men's silhouettes—in fact, they had been already.

A few men's samples were shown on the big male models of the day, like Tony Spinelli, in the designer's fashion shows in the early 1970s. These samples were strictly showpieces to dress up the runway, but retailers like Saks Fifth Avenue and Bloomingdale's would clamor for menswear after seeing them, each offering to finance exclusive collections.

"In 1975 . . . we started talking very seriously about doing menswear," Banks said. "I always pushed Calvin to show men's things in the show, and Charles, the showman, wanted to have men's because he thought it would make the show more dramatic."

At the urging of the design staff, Klein and Schwartz started negotiations with a man named Irving Selbst from a company named Bond Clothing. While it looked like a done deal, the negotiations fell apart at the eleventh hour over the issue of royalties.

The company was back to square one as far as menswear was concerned, until a Frenchman named Maurice Bidermann came calling.

Regardless of his nationality, Bidermann was nonetheless a garmento, akin to the Seventh Avenue variety Klein and Schwartz were growing adept at handling. While the duo had successfully negotiated a number of licenses for themselves, getting their terms, they had met their match in Bidermann.

In dealing with the top design houses of France, Bidermann found that designers would give up design and quality control in exchange for a higher royalty rate. However, Schwartz and Klein, who proved to be even tougher negotiators on the control issue, would not budge. A deal was eventually struck where the design company granted Bidermann the license to produce a complete menswear collection—suits, sport coats, topcoats, trousers, shirts, sweaters, leisure wear, ties, belts, hosiery, and underwear—some of which would debut in fall of 1978.

No sector of the fashion industry is more affected by fashion cycles than jeanswear. When it is hot, there are billions and billions of dollars out there to be picked up. When it is off cycle, you're lucky if you can sell a pair of replacement dungarees to a farmer. However, no fashion product is more American, and as an up-and-coming American designer, Calvin Klein couldn't resist trying his hand at designing jeans.

Calvin Klein jeans debuted in 1976 and were an immediate flop. Designed and manufactured in-house at the company, these jeans, priced at $50, were more expensive than Gloria Vanderbilt's, and customers complained that they didn't fit.

In retrospect, Klein should have taken the debacle at the fashion show in which they debuted as an omen.

The jeans were going to be sold at Bloomingdale's, which

had just opened a Calvin Klein shop. To support the shop, Klein agreed to do a fashion show at the store where the jeans would debut.

Instead of sending the jeans to an actual manufacturer that had the right equipment, "we had made the jeans in the sample room," Banks recalled. Consequently, they were a little less than pristine.

"As the model walked down the runway with this stitched Calvin Klein label on her back pocket, it started to come off," Banks said, mortified. "It didn't come off completely, but it started to."

Needless to say, the jeans didn't sell, and Klein retreated, until a man named Peter King approached him one night at 4 A.M. on the dance floor at Studio 54. The man suggested that Klein could make at least $1 million a year by licensing his name for jeans to a company called Puritan Fashions, a maker of moderately priced dresses that was run by Carl Rosen. Klein was leaving the next day for a business trip to Frankfurt, Germany, and while the dollar figure excited him, he put the offer out of his mind after he alerted Schwartz to expect a call.

By the time Calvin returned from his trip, he had forgotten about the late-night conversation until Schwartz reminded him. "I think we've got a live one here," he said.

Unbeknownst to Klein and Schwartz, they weren't Rosen's first choice.

"Before Carl went to Calvin, he went to [Pierre] Cardin in Paris and met with Mr. Cardin," DeMarco said. "And Carl, being the obnoxious individual that he was, got down with Mr. Cardin, and said he was going to make him a millionaire," which annoyed Cardin to no end.

"With what?" Cardin asked.

"With jeans—designer jeans," Rosen replied.

"Cardin did not like the man. He looked Carl in the face and he said, 'Mr. Rosen? There are no cowboys in Paris,' and walked out of the room," DeMarco said. "Three weeks after that, Carl signed Calvin Klein."

The resulting deal between Calvin Klein and Puritan's Carl Rosen went down in history as one of the greatest licensing deals of all time. The strict specifications that Schwartz negotiated would become legendary in the industry and would allow the Calvin Klein name to be protected, not exploited.

In addition to a $1 million signing bonus, the contract would pay Calvin Klein a minimum of $1 million every year for the life of the contract, with a royalty rate of $1 per pair of jeans sold, and with a cost-of-living increase built in. In exchange, Klein would design the jeans and create the advertising Puritan would pay to produce and place.

As Klein's business was on the brink of being transformed, his life was being subjected to a shock. Klein was devoted to his daughter Marci. Though she lived with her mother, he spent time with her regularly and would do just about anything she asked. One morning, as the 11-year-old girl was on her way to school, she was lured away by a former babysitter who said Klein was sick and needed her. The kidnapping and Marci's subsequent rescue by her father and the FBI was top news in New York City and across the country. Authorities originally suspected the kidnapping was a publicity stunt by the designer to draw attention to the launch of his jeans. However, the capture of the suspected kidnappers, Christine Ransay, Dominique Ransay, and Cecil "Mousie" Wiggins, proved otherwise.

Calvin Klein jeans, manufactured by Puritan, hit the market at precisely the right time, becoming the brand that led the designer jeans craze. It was the combination of the right name on the right product at the right time that allowed retailers to stack them high and let them fly. More than 200,000 pairs were sold right out of the gate in 1978. In the first year, Calvin Klein jeans came in number two to Gloria Vanderbilt. Puritan had $80 million in sales that year, one-third of which came from Calvin Klein jeans. Schwartz and Klein, flush with royalty payments, immediately bought 7 percent of Puritan's outstanding shares on the stock market.

To support the image of Calvin Klein jeans, the company embarked on its first advertising campaign. The company decided that the ideal space to have would be the billboard high above Times Square at 45th and Broadway.

Klein hired photographer Charles Tracy to do the shoot with the bold, blond Patti Hansen, one of the first super-models, who later married the Rolling Stones guitarist Keith Richards. On the shoot, Hansen was horsing around to unspectacular results until she made her way to the floor with her back to the camera.

The result was a 900- by 200-foot image of the brassy blond with her butt sticking out for all to see. On the right pocket, in all its glory, was the Calvin Klein label.

"Patti's a really hot, incredible girl," Klein said of the photo that showed her tawny mane in midair behind her.

This billboard, which cost Puritan all of $60,000 to rent for a year, stayed up for four years, driving sales and infuriating feminist Gloria Steinem and women's groups, until a 15-year-old model/actress named Brooke took its place, making them look back on Patti Hansen's backside fondly.

By 1980, every designer and celebrity was jumping on the jeans bandwagon. Besides Gloria Vanderbilt and Calvin Klein, companies like Bonjour, Sasson, Zena, and Jordache were competing for designer jeans customers. Klein and Puritan's Rosen realized they would have to up the ante and use television advertising to differentiate their jeans.

Longtime fashion photographer Richard Avedon and copywriter Doon Arbus, daughter of famed photographer Diane Arbus, were hired to create the advertisements that would feature a nubile, young model named Brooke Shields. The 15-year-old Shields had been working since she was cast as an Ivory Snow baby at 11 months. Her first starring role in a feature film, playing the prepubescent daughter of a prostitute in Louis Malle's *Pretty Baby,* changed the way people viewed this young model. In this role, Shields created a controversy not unlike the one the Calvin Klein jeans campaign would generate.

Avedon and Arbus created a series of commercials that revolved around the jeans, treating them as a character.

"Reading is to the mind what Calvins are to the body," Shields said suggestively.

"I've got seven Calvins in my closet, and if they could talk, I'd be ruined," she said with mock horror.

"Whenever I get some money, I buy Calvins. And if there's any left, I pay the rent," she said, irresponsibly.

And, perhaps the most famous commercial, which can be recited by millions even today, more than 20 years after it first aired, "Do you know what comes between me and my Calvins? Nothing."

These advertisements did their job. In the week following their debut, the company sold an impressive 400,000 pairs of jeans, double what was sold at the launch in 1978. More important, the Calvin Klein image—edgy, clever, sexual, and usually controversial—was born, as was the public outcry that allowed this company to maximize its media exposure.

The world started turning on Klein slowly, with some television stations backing off airing the commercials, or showing them only late at night. However, when the New York City stations got involved, the media jumped on the story, citing psychologists, women's groups, and educators, who claimed the ads were doing everything from glorifying sex to conveying hidden messages about homosexuality.

Klein and photographer Richard Avedon had intended to do something different and interesting. "We were using Brooke as an actress; she was playing different roles: a liberated woman, a teenager, a vamp," Klein defended, claiming that it was not any different from *Vogue* using Brooke as the model for expensive haute couture.

However, he added that advertising jeans in general is challenging because it's all been done before. "The only way . . . is by not focusing on the product," he said. And it worked to the tune of 2 million pairs a month sold in the period after the ads hit the airwaves. Calvin Klein took in royalties of $12.5 million in 1980 from the sale of jeans alone.

CHAPTER 4

Booming Boxers and Briefs

Perhaps the reason nothing came between Brooke Shields and her jeans was simple—Calvin Klein underwear didn't exist.

However, Calvin Klein was making efforts to remedy this situation. In his quest to dress men from head to toe, underwear was a category that intrigued Klein. The sex, drugs, and disco environment Klein was living in glorified well-toned bodies, both male and female. While nudity was all around the Studio 54 scene, Klein believed bodies looked better when something was left to the imagination—he preferred underwear.

"Why don't you do a line of underwear?" top model Janice Dickinson claims she said in the company of Klein and model Iman, after a long, hard-partying night at Studio 54 in the early 1980s. "Just put your name on it. I bet it'll sell." A spark shot across his face, but that was the last mention of it. "He didn't say anything," she said.

While Dickinson believes she gave Klein the idea for creating his line of namesake underwear, its origins were more organic.

"A designer who designs for men should do everything for men," Klein said.

The look the model saw on Klein's face was probably shock that she'd read his mind, as Klein had been looking at tapping into the lucrative market for men's and boy's underwear—a whopping $2 billion in sales in 1981.

Most men's underwear at that time was sold three to a pack at a promotional price. Men bought underwear when they needed to, but usually a wife, mother, or girlfriend purchased these necessary objects that were as basic as white bread.

With one campaign, Jockey and former Baltimore Oriole pitcher Jim Palmer changed that perception. The handsome and fit Palmer was shown wearing nothing but underwear, briefs in fact, in a locker room in the company's ad campaign. Not only did this advertisement appeal to the women who were buying the underwear, boosting Jockey's sales by 10 percent, but it created a whole new ball game where standards were concerned. And Klein, the king of the sexy ad campaign, had to get in the game.

The company chose Bloomingdale's to test its briefs, boxer shorts, bikinis, and T-shirts in late summer 1982, as the store was considered the best testing ground for new men's items. In addition, the retailer and its fashion director Kal Ruttenstein had been supportive of the designer since the beginning, being the first to devote space to an in-store shop for Calvin Klein.

In the first five days, Calvin Klein underwear sold more than 400 dozen pieces; by the end of the second week, sales were $65,000, with white briefs accounting for the bulk of these sales.

Priced at $14.50, the Calvin Klein three-pack was considerably more expensive than the Bloomingdale's brand, priced at $8, yet men showed no resistance to the price. The Calvin Klein brand had enough clout to succeed in doing the impossible—getting the American male to care about the brand of something few ever see. It also established a base price point for the designer's wares that was affordable to many. When you wanted to be a part of the Calvin Klein lifestyle, three for $14.50 is slightly easier on the wallet than $40 jeans.

Even more telling was that the underwear, created under the Bidermann license, was manufactured in the same factory as Jockey's white briefs and Yves Saint Laurent's licensed underwear. The only difference between these three brands was the name on the waistband and the price—surprisingly, Calvin Klein was priced higher.

"I wouldn't have done underwear if I didn't think I could make a valid contribution," Klein said. "We emphasized the basic white brief to establish the fact that we're in the business. I wanted the underwear to feel comfortable and fit properly . . . those were the most important things."

The introduction of the men's underwear was supported by a substantial advertising campaign, with a budget of $500,000. And, of course, the suggestive advertising campaign for Calvin Klein underwear convinced America that plain white underwear could be incredibly sexy.

While more overt than the Jockey ads, Klein also chose an athlete to star in the advertisements. Former Olympic pole vaulter Tim Hintinaus's long, lithe, muscular body was shown reclining against a white building with the sky in the background. The contrast of the white and blue against the sheen of his tanned skin made for an arresting image. The detail and shadows hinting to what was inside the underwear added to its allure.

For the first time in Calvin Klein history, its advertisements inspired crime.

The underwear ads were so popular that over 50 bus shelters containing the ads were broken into and the posters stolen. "The posters incite vandalism," Klein said.

It was ultimately the product consumers were after, which allowed the company to project sales of $4 million for men's underwear in its first year at retail.

"That it's selling is wonderful," said Bob Garey, then president of Calvin Klein Menswear. More important, "Getting the customer back the second time is what will make the Calvin Klein underwear business."

To make that conversion, Klein had to give customers a reason to buy season after season. While Klein personally espoused a philosophy of neutrals for himself—black, white, khaki, and brown—color was the solution for the underwear business.

In addition to the black, white, and gray unmentionables the company originally offered, subsequent seasons included an array of colors—purple, navy, oatmeal, even red—which turned something basic into fashion objects to be bought every season.

Calvin Klein turned its attention to women's underwear next, but instead of simplifying something that was basic to begin with, the designer created women's underwear that resembled men's briefs, in cotton knit, some complete with a functional fly.

"Men's briefs are hot" on women, Klein said. "I like the idea of a woman wearing something that's masculine." Klein's idea of modern underwear for women included briefs, bikinis, string bikinis, and boxer shorts, all with a fly.

Klein supported the debut of the women's underwear with an advertising campaign that was similar in feel to the men's campaign. The campaign showed an androgynous-looking woman in bikini briefs lying down with her back arched and her tank top pulled up to expose one nipple. While the company had to airbrush the nipple out before the ads could be placed in certain magazines and in bus shelters, it was clear Calvin Klein was the pioneer of shocking ads that have become so commonplace today.

As with the men's underwear, the women's sales were through the roof. The company originally projected sales of $18 million to $20 million for the first year. However, after 200 stores reordered their entire stock within three months of delivery, the estimates were bumped up to $48 million. Ultimately, underwear racked up sales of $70 million in 1984, based in part on its sexy advertising.

Expectations for women's underwear were originally as high as they were for the designer jeans business. The combination of a quality product with the Calvin Klein label at an affordable price once again proved irresistible to consumers.

The stunning success of the women's underwear business was something that Schwartz and Klein smartly realized they couldn't handle themselves. The duo started shopping the division as an asset to be sold, not just licensed as the men's underwear was to Bidermann. In August 1984, the women's underwear business was sold to Kayser-Roth Corporation, a division of Gulf & Western, for $8.3 million in cash and the potential for $2.9 million in future payments, with Klein keeping artistic control over the design, production, and advertising of the line. In addition to buying the underwear business, Kayser-Roth also signed licenses to create Calvin Klein hosiery and sleepwear.

And, in a twist neither Schwartz nor Klein could anticipate, their business with Kayser-Roth, in fact all of Kayser-Roth, was sold the following year to Wickes Companies.

Parent Gulf + Western was refocusing on its entertainment and communications divisions, which included Paramount Pictures and Simon & Schuster publishing. The sale, which included licenses with Liz Claiborne and Jonathan Logan as well as Klein, netted Gulf + Western $1 billion in cash and allowed it sell $90 million in long-term debt.

The amazing success of Calvin Klein underwear led to imitators and knockoffs, but Klein kept reinventing the product season after season, allowing it to remain the dominant brand. In no time at all, Calvin Klein underwear became part of the fabric of American culture, even being immortalized on film in 1985 in Michael J. Fox's *Back to the Future*.

"I've never seen red underwear before, Calvin," said Lea Thompson's character Lorraine to Michael J. Fox's time-traveling Marty McFly.

"Calvin? Why are you calling me Calvin?" he asked.

"Well, isn't that your name—Calvin Klein? It's written in your underwear."

CHAPTER 5

The Cost of Business

C alvin Klein was enjoying success at every turn. Besides its newfound triumph with underwear, the designer jeans frenzy reached a crescendo in the early 1980s, with Calvin Klein jeans leading the way. Millions of pairs of jeans with the distinctive red lettering on a white label—14 different styles for men, women, and children—graced the backsides of people coast to coast, from schoolgirls to socialites.

Calvin Klein, Barry Schwartz, and Puritan's Carl Rosen were all enjoying the spoils of this business. In 1982, jeans licensee Puritan paid Klein and Schwartz about $14 million in royalties, while Rosen's company was transformed from a high-debt, low-profit-margin manufacturer to a low-debt, high-profit operation that sourced manufacturing in many places.

Though there was plenty to go around, Klein and Schwartz were growing to resent Rosen and the fact that Calvin Klein jeans accounted for 94 percent of the company's almost $250 million in sales. Klein believed the garmento was growing wealthy on his (Klein's) name, while Rosen believed the duo from the Bronx was nothing without him. It was a situation where both sides thought they were being taken advantage of by the other. Klein and Schwartz vowed to do something about it, but were biding their time until the right opportunity presented itself.

However, in 1983, the happy days of designer jeans ground to a halt. Disco was dead and with it went the popularity of jeans in general. The company did what it could to combat the lagging sales by toying with the washes and treatments to which the denim was subjected. Stonewashed jeans, with a light blue color and a worn feel, were first debuted during this time. Then the company tried the opposite extreme, with jeans that were overdyed in colors like red, purple, and black. It was no use—the consumer had moved on.

In the 1980s, pop culture was fragmented into a number of camps, with two of the more prominent ones being romantic new wave, represented by English performers like Adam Ant and Spandau Ballet, and sugary sweet bubblegum pop, represented by the likes of Toni Basil and Lisa Lisa & Cult Jam. With ruffled pirate shirts and brightly colored pedal pushers in vogue, denim was dead. Teenagers, in particular, had taken to wearing "parachute pants," combat-like trousers made of a type of nylon that resembled the material used to make parachutes.

One year earlier, Rosen, Puritan's chairman and president, had been diagnosed with cancer. Conscious of his mortality, Rosen stepped up his efforts to educate his heir apparent—son Andrew, then age 26—in the ways of the company, and he actually moved Andrew's desk into his office so that the younger Rosen could witness and learn from his father's every move and conversation.

Andrew Rosen fit the stereotypical dilettante. Growing

up, he spent the bulk of his time playing golf and clowning around in the electric golf carts on the courses. He attended numerous prep schools and colleges, only to skip classes and play even more golf, never even completing his degree at the University of Miami before starting to work for his father.

In March 1983, after his short tutorial in how to run the business, Carl Rosen and the company board he controlled named Andrew president and chief operating officer of Puritan, much to the chagrin of Klein and Schwartz. The gauntlet had been thrown, and Klein and Schwartz knew they had no choice but to buy Puritan Fashion when the elder Rosen passed away.

"We disagreed about everything," Klein explained. "I was trying to sell the name Calvin Klein and what it stood for, but that was not the philosophy of the jeans company. The Rosens actually believed the tremendous success they had was something they had created." The arrogance didn't bother Klein when the bucks were rolling in, but the times had changed and were about to get worse.

The first sign of trouble began with Carl Rosen's death in August 1983. The company's board voted to give the title of chief executive officer to Andrew a mere three weeks later, though, as one board member put it, "Andrew would be the first to acknowledge he doesn't have the experience to sit at the head of the company and run it unilaterally." Even so, he was heading up a $250 million company.

Klein and Schwartz didn't sit back and wait for Andrew to fail; they were already covertly meeting with their bankers at Manufacturers Hanover Trust Company to arrange for the $60 to $100 million it would cost to buy Puritan Fashions outright. Throughout Calvin Klein's growth and expansion, the duo had relied almost exclusively on this bank for financing, and its debt had grown to be quite substantial.

Each successive bit of news emerging from Puritan after Andrew Rosen took the helm reinforced Klein and
Schwartz's resolve. In October 1983, Rosen downgraded the
company's earnings outlook for the year. Blaming "unexpectedly slow sales of its crucial Calvin Klein jeans line," he
said the company's earnings would be closer to the previous
year's earnings than to the previously projected increase of
$1 per share. That was the last straw for Klein and Schwartz.

"Profits were sliding—in just one quarter, revenues fell 61
percent—and the people managing Puritan disagreed with
me on how the company should be run," Klein explained.

"Andrew is a nice man, but Puritan is a $250 million com-
pany. . . . We believed we could manage the company a hell
of a lot better than Andrew," Klein said. "I have no personal
animosity toward anyone in the Rosen family, but no 27-
year-old had the experience to run a company that does a
quarter of a billion dollars a year in sales."

On November 14, 1983, the duo made an offer to acquire
the outstanding shares of Puritan Fashions for $16.50 each, a
deal valued at about $60 million. This announcement was
the first time they publicly said they lacked confidence in
Andrew Rosen's ability to run the company. While a Puritan
spokesman said the company was taken by surprise, Klein's
camp was confident. Schwartz was "hopeful" about meeting
with Rosen, and a Klein company spokesman said, "We
don't anticipate financing to be a problem at all."

The next two weeks were a frenzy of meetings and negotiations for all involved. Klein and Schwartz were very clear
in their offer that they wanted a quick decision from Puritan's board. And when the board said it was deferring action
on Calvin Klein's proposal, Klein struck back.

Klein and Schwartz fully intended to acquire Puritan—it
was a matter of pride and controlling their brand at that
point. If the board couldn't come to terms in a friendly

manner, the street-savvy duo from the Bronx made it clear they would break out their true colors and offer $15.50 per share in a hostile takeover bid.

"We have concluded that we have no real choice but to proceed on our own if a mutual transaction cannot be achieved," Schwartz said.

Further, Klein said, "The direct and indirect costs to us of proceeding in this manner, coupled with the absence of any form of representations incident to a negotiated transaction, require us to lower the price we would be willing to pay."

The decision now lay squarely on the Rosen family, who controlled between 11 and 15 percent of the company's outstanding shares. While Andrew wanted to fight, his mother, Carl's widow Shirley, wanted out, which led the family to sell.

There was some backroom dealing, during which the final negotiations resulted in a purchase price of $17.50 per share and a guaranteed position for Andrew Rosen in the new Puritan, to be henceforth known as Calvin Klein Sport, a division of the newly renamed Calvin Klein, Inc. The deal was finalized in late March 1984, with Calvin Klein paying approximately $75 million to acquire Puritan's shares and outstanding debt, putting his company in even greater debt to Manufacturers Hanover Trust. However, in the end, Klein and Schwartz's desire to control Puritan would end up costing significantly more than $17.50 a share.

CHAPTER 6

Obsession

While the introduction of Obsession would be one of the most successful fragrance launches in history, Calvin Klein was originally behind the curve when it came to developing a fragrance. It drove him crazy.

Like the European fashion houses of Chanel or Dior, Klein knew his company needed a fragrance to round out its offerings to the American public. And it didn't help his fixation to see other American designers going where he wanted to go, literally.

Calvin Klein had an obsession with Halston. The designer was as big and bold-faced a name as the celebrities he courted; stars like Liza Minelli and Liz Taylor constantly orbited his world.

Once, when Klein was lunching with fashion publicist Eleanor Lambert, who ran her own agency as well as the Coty Awards, he saw a commotion being made over Halston and vowed that he, too, would be treated like a celebrity.

"I'm good-looking and rich and I move in fast circles," Klein said.

"He was fascinated with Halston," Lambert said. "He wanted to be like him and he did everything he could to show he belonged with the Studio 54 set," drinking, allegedly using drugs, and staying out all night with an entourage that included Brooke Shields and assorted models, Steve Rubell and Ian Schrager, and eventually Bianca Jagger.

"The biggest thing . . . was that there was a huge defection from Halston's camp—Bianca Jagger," said a fashion insider. "Halston dressed Bianca. Bianca lived in Halston's house." However, "she got tired of whatever was happening," in Halston's camp. "Calvin, in a moment, a gigantic fashion moment, started to dress her."

"Steve Rubell was running interference," between the designers, "but in the end, Calvin ended up in this very enviable position of being the new, hot kid in town. And don't forget, Calvin was very, very handsome," said the insider, which only added to his allure.

But getting the girl and being a part of the in crowd was not enough for the designer. Halston had introduced his signature crisp, sophisticated fragrance in the 1970s and it became a must-have for women—an immediate success. Touted as the most successful fragrance to be introduced on the market in years, the ubiquitous scent was expected to generate $100 million in sales by its second year.

Combined with his worship of Halston, the success of Halston's fragrance was almost too much for Klein to take.

The fragrance and cosmetics industry is one that is rife with potential profits, as the products themselves are inexpensive to make. Fragrance is made primarily of low-cost alcohol, lipstick is made primarily of wax. Once a beauty product is created, there is enormous opportunity for profit through margins that put the apparel industry to shame.

However, the risks that beauty manufacturers have to take are much greater. The product's creation, packaging, marketing, and advertising incur seemingly incredible costs. The development of a fragrance starts at no less than $10 million and can soar to more than $50 million to establish a brand. However, if the product beats the odds—six out of seven launches fail—the potential for return is limitless, easily reaching millions and millions of dollars.

Beauty products serve as an affordable way to buy into the designer's lifestyle. Similar to Calvin Klein underwear or even jeans, a fragrance product priced below $50 is a small luxury item that consumers will regularly spend their hard-earned money on.

"In the history of the world, there've only been a few thousand women who've worn a Chanel couture gown," explained designer Jeffrey Banks. "But in the history of the world there are tens of millions of women who've had Chanel perfume, Chanel makeup, or Chanel sunglasses. Those are the accessible ways of getting a piece of Chanel."

At that time, Klein and Schwartz were just starting to use licensing deals as sources of revenue. They hadn't quite learned that licensing the company's name to an expert in a field was a low-risk, low-cost way to make what they wanted to. Still not satisfied with their successes, these scrappy men from the Bronx viewed licensed products as a vehicle that allowed others to get rich from their name and the brand they had built.

Though there were offers from the big beauty companies, Schwartz and Klein weighed their options for cosmetic licenses. However, the idea of keeping all the profits, not just a percentage, and control over the product and advertising, clouded their vision. They decided to start their own company in 1977—Calvin Klein Cosmetics—and operate it as a division of Calvin Klein Industries.

They hired a beauty industry veteran, Stanley Kohlenberg, to run the division. Klein had met Kohlenberg through his wife, a nurse who was treating Klein on a day he was particularly ticked off about Halston's success. Klein's kvetching led to an introduction to Kohlenberg, then president of a division of Revlon. Kohlenberg left the beauty giant to sign on with Klein and Schwartz shortly thereafter.

It was decided that the company would develop its first fragrance, called Calvin Klein, with the help of International Flavors & Fragrances, Inc. (IFF), an industry leader. The problem was that neither Klein nor Schwartz knew what they wanted.

"I bought every fragrance in the United States, masked them, and sprayed him with three a day," Kohlenberg said of Klein. "He hated everything but musk."

Still, the company had to forge ahead in a prompt fashion, as another designer was also getting into the fragrance game.

Ralph Lauren, a former classmate at PS 80 in the Bronx, was on the verge of launching two fragrances, one for men and one for women, simultaneously. Instead of licensing his name, Lauren had entered into a partnership with Warner Communications to create a separate company that would create and market the new Lauren fragrances.

The Klein and Lauren camps smelled and rejected fragrances from the same IFF labs without much luck, when a leader finally emerged. Klein assembled a group of employees and outside colleagues to test it, including Baron de Gunzburg and *New York Times*'s Carrie Donovan, an early fan of Klein's who was later made famous playing the fashion authority in the Old Navy ads. With one wrinkle of the baron's nose, Klein dismissed the scent and they were back to square one.

Klein finally settled on a fragrance that originated in a small custom *parfumerie* in Paris, while the former contender was released to be used by other IFF customers.

Meanwhile, Lauren had beat Klein to the punch, securing Bloomingdale's, the home of Klein's first foray into jeanswear, for the launch of Lauren for women and Polo for men. The store offered Klein the week following the Lauren launches, but the company chose to go elsewhere.

"Calvin couldn't break after Ralph, so we went to Saks," Kohlenberg said.

Saks Fifth Avenue wanted to build a promotional campaign around the young, good-looking designer, but he balked at doing anything similar to what Bloomingdale's was doing with Lauren. The sexy new advertising campaign that featured a couple showing lots of skin in several stages of undress would have to do.

Once the fragrances hit the stores, the shit hit the fan. Klein's didn't sell, while Lauren's sales went crazy.

"A week later, Barry called me screaming," Kohlenberg said, his preferred method of communicating his anger.

"Have you smelled it?" Kohlenberg asked.

"This is our fragrance!" Schwartz screamed back. "Lauren" was the leading contender that had been rejected by the Klein camp. It is still a top-selling fragrance worldwide, regardless of the baron's wrinkled nose.

Meanwhile, Calvin Klein, the fragrance, never took hold. It didn't matter that the advertisements were classic, sexy Calvin style—the fragrance was dead on arrival, giving Klein and Schwartz their first taste of failure.

For Schwartz, who had experienced nothing but overnight successes up to this point, waiting for the cosmetics line to develop a following was impossible—he was too impatient.

"We were making a lot of money," in other areas, Schwartz said. But "we were pouring a lot of money into it. It was draining."

He abruptly pulled the plug on the fragrance and cosmetics business in November 1979, firing staff, stopping production midcycle, canceling airline tickets, and reneging on contracts. Many employees in the field were left with thousands of dollars of unpaid wages and expenses.

"It didn't work because I did it with my own company and I didn't know what I was doing," Klein explained. "I lost a lot of money," an estimated $4 million.

A funny thing happened a month after Klein and Schwartz pulled the plug on Calvin Klein Cosmetics—someone wanted to buy the company, lock, stock, and barrel.

A midwesterner named Robert Taylor had read about the plight of the company and believed there was money to be made selling beauty products under the Calvin Klein brand name, by the right company—*his*.

Taylor's outfit, Minnetonka Industries, was an unlikely candidate, as it was a beauty company only in the broadest sense of the word. Minnetonka made its name (and a fortune) on the Softsoap brand of liquid hand soap and followed up that success with the first pump-dispensed toothpaste, called Check-up. It also sold such sundry brands as Village Bath, LaCosta Spa, and Institute Swiss soaps and bath products.

However, there was not a luxury item or designer brand in his stable, something that made Schwartz and Klein balk at first. However, their desire to earn back any money lost on the cosmetics debacle overrode their skepticism.

Negotiations started, and the parties had reached agreement on most issues. Taylor bought basically everything associated with Calvin Klein Cosmetics in exchange for $506,000 in cash and 30,000 shares of Minnetonka stock. They agreed that Klein would have total control over any product the company made that carried his name. However, the royalty rate was a sticking point.

Taylor was offering 5 percent on a five-year deal that was renewable in perpetuity, provided certain sales guarantees were met. Schwartz, forgetting or perhaps ignoring the fact that he was being bailed out, insisted on more, in his less than cordial style of communicating.

"I don't give a shit what you say!" Barry shrieked. "Five percent is not acceptable."

"You'll take the 5 percent or I'm packing up and leaving for Minnesota tonight," Taylor said quietly, shocked that he'd been yelled at that way.

The deal was done, and Taylor walked away with more than he bargained for, though not, initially, in a good way.

When Schwartz was running the company, he insisted on no returns of product, which is the opposite of the service that department stores normally expected. When he pulled the plug, Schwartz abandoned literally hundreds of thousands of dollars' worth of product. Once Taylor signed on, Schwartz expected him to collect on those outstanding receivables and split the proceeds. However, Taylor, attempting to reestablish good relations with these stores, took the returns and even paid outstanding sales commissions to their employees. In total, Taylor figured Klein and Schwartz owed him $1.2 million in reimbursements, something the duo from the Bronx hotly contested all the way to arbitration, which was settled in 1983 with Klein and Schwartz owing Taylor $668,352, all the while working within a contemptuous relationship.

. . .

The fashion tide was turning toward androgyny in the early 1980s, as women's wear took on the proportions of menswear. Broad shoulders, narrow waists and hips, dress shirts, and trouser suits were showing up on women's runways, and they looked surprisingly sexy, particularly on mannequins with cropped hair. While not credited with starting this trend, Calvin Klein's women's man-style underwear, complete with a functional fly, gave it a kick in the backside.

The designer needed a model to complete his picture—a signature model who would convey the image of the modern minimalism he espoused. However, the one he wanted, a lithe model from South Africa named Jose Borain (pronounced Jo-see), was on the verge of signing an exclusive contract with Klein's sometime rival Ralph Lauren, something that spurred him into action.

While agents from Click, Borain's management, were negotiating with Lauren, they allowed her to work for Klein in editorial shoots and showroom work. Strategizing that this would goad Lauren into signing a deal with the agency on the model's behalf faster, it backfired. Klein used his burgeoning relationship with Borain to negotiate an exclusive deal directly with the model herself.

Klein agreed to pay the model $1 million over three years for 100 days work a year, plus an additional $3,000 for any extra days Klein needed her. In exchange, Borain was required to maintain her hairstyle and color and physical appearance, weighing no less than 120 pounds and no more than 130. This was a substantial and unusual deal for a model to be given, as exclusives of this type, while used by beauty companies, hadn't been used by designers up to this point.

Borain was the perfect embodiment of Klein's designs. She was tall, lean, and athletic, yet she had the hint of womanly curves that complemented Klein's clothes. While not a traditional beauty, her distinctive looks were strong, yet at times sweet, bordering on handsome. She was Calvin Klein's modern woman seen most often in some stage of undress for underwear, clothing, and later, for the fragrance Obsession.

With the financial feud behind them, Schwartz and Klein were compelled to go forward with the spirit of the licensing agreement with Taylor. However, any attempts Taylor had made up to that point to work with the duo, and particularly Klein, were met with stony silences and open hostility. Klein let it be known that if the relationship was to go forward, Taylor had to find someone he (Klein) approved of to run Calvin Klein Cosmetics.

Taylor recruited a young executive from Bloomingdale's named Robin Burns, and while she had no experience running a company, her reputation as a tough, intuitive leader proceeded her. The only problem was that Taylor hired Burns without consulting Klein, which immediately put Klein on the defensive, predisposed to dislike Burns.

Robin Burns was not a woman to be taken lightly. The petite blond powerhouse had a background in competition—in both figure skating and skiing—which she honed while growing up in Colorado. Burns rose through the ranks at Bloomingdale's to head its beauty department before she was 30 and was not going to let Klein's bad attitude get in the way of her plans for the company.

While the designer would not schedule a meeting with her or even take her calls, Burns went to those around Klein to try to get a toehold. Kelly Rector, Klein's design assistant, girlfriend, and future wife, rose to the bait and eventually served as Burns's conduit.

Rector met with Burns over lunch, and once she heard Burns's ambitious plans for a sexy new fragrance, she gave her a rousing endorsement, causing Klein to come around.

Minnetonka desperately wanted to get a fragrance on the market to replace the toothless Calvin Klein perfume, which, though still on the market, was wilting on the vine. To create the new fragrance, Burns was not fooling around. She hired Ann Gottlieb, a fragrance consultant, sometimes referred to as a "nose," and asked fragrance houses for samples.

A firm named Rourge-Bertram DuPont hit the jackpot on the first pull. Their fragrance was described as a combination of "mandarin, bergamot and a subtle green note with jasmine, rose and orange blossoms." Midnotes are a blend of "coriander, taget and armoise," over a base of "amber mingled with oak moss."

"The fragrance is not a floral; it's not outdoorsy and woodsy. It's a very sensual scent and yet, one can wear it day or night," Klein explained. "Even a man can wear it."

The golden liquid was a hit with both the Klein and the Minnetonka camps, so much so that Minnetonka committed $17 million for marketing and advertisement and Klein committed to go on the road for its launch.

First though, the packaging had to be decided upon, and Klein was adamant on the direction. "I collect tortoiseshell, blonde tortoiseshell especially," which is where the shade and feel for the bottle's cap came from. The actual squat shape of the bottle reflected Klein's collection of tantric sculptures and Indian prayer stones. "They're all a part of me," he said.

Once the name evolved from the vulgar Climax to its final Obsession, Klein wholeheartedly jumped on the promotional bandwagon, peppering every sound bite he gave with references to the fragrance.

Klein said he was "obsessed with perfection, obsessed with work, obsessed with offering people new things. I know a lot of people who are obsessed with their career." He noted, "The sexual connotation was in the background."

He explained, "When one makes love, there is a certain scent that we give off. I think it's very sensual—that's the scent of Obsession."

While Obsession was a nice enough fragrance, it was the advertising for the perfume that made it so irresistible. The company created both television and print advertising that pushed conventionality, as well as introducing the idea of ambisexuality. The commercials featured signature model Jose Borain in a series of Dali-esque vignettes with three men—a boy, a contemporary, and an older man—and also an older woman.

"She loved me and she's gone," said the boy, full of woe, as Borain flits around the set. "Did I invent her? The secrets in her twilight eyes . . . the whispers at my bedside . . . her arms . . . her mouth . . . her amber hair and, oh, the smell of it. She's deep in my blood, the only woman I'll ever love."

"Love is child's play once you've known Obsession," she whispered, knowingly.

"Ah, the smell of it."

The ads, directed by famed fashion photographer Richard Avedon and filmed by cinematographer Nestor Almendros, were scandalous, not only to the puzzled consumers who watched them, but also to the fragrance industry. The use of the word *smell* was revolutionary in an industry that preferred euphemisms like *aroma, fragrance,* or *scent.*

The print advertising was less abstract, but more overt in its sexy imagery. Shot by Bruce Weber, the campaign again featured three men with Jose, all naked, with intertwined limbs shot in such a way that it's hard to tell which belongs to whom. The final images were shown in a grainy blue sepia tone which added a gritty, after-dark edge, inspired, in part, by its Puerto Vallarta, Mexico, location.

"We were in a warm place," Klein explained. "People would go swimming at night and it sort of happened from there."

"My work is my obsession," Klein admitted. "I must admit that I do have fun fooling around with these ads. I don't think what I do is pornographic. . . . You walk a fine line, especially in advertising, if you try to do something sensual. Everyone who creates walks a little bit on the edge."

Sales were projected to be $40 million in first year, with Klein making personal appearances in cities like San Francisco, Chicago, Dallas, and Washington, D.C., to make the introduction.

The campaign's whistle-stop tour was a challenge for Klein, who regardless of his success lacked confidence and had a deep-rooted dislike for *real* customers. He was still the shy guy from Mosholu Parkway who wouldn't even sit for his high school picture.

"This is my first time in Dallas and I'm frightened," he admitted to a *Dallas Morning News* reporter. "Because I've never been here, I don't know what to expect. I think there will probably be no one downstairs," for his appearance at Neiman Marcus's Prestonwood store.

The designer was pleasantly surprised with a waiting crowd of more than 400—most of whom stood in line for over an hour waiting for an autograph. It was crazed consumers like those who helped the fragrance break $30 million in wholesale sales in its first year.

.   .   .

The company followed the fragrance launch with the launch of Obsession body products—oils, dusting powder, lotion, soap—one year later, as well as the launch of Obsession for men. It also launched a new, more provocative advertising campaign that, unbelievably, featured even more skin.

The main image featured a man kissing a woman's bare torso, complete with exposed nipple in a jolt of intimacy.

"We're now making Obsession-scented products for the body, so it only seems natural to show a woman's body and show it in the most beautiful way we can," Klein said.

Appropriately, *Time* magazine crowned Klein "America's undisputed pacesetter in turning out erotic ads and commercials."

CHAPTER 7

Calvin's Kelly Girl

alvin Klein was looking for a design assistant in 1981. Though he had a battery of stylists working with him behind the scenes, including Zack Carr, who had been with Klein from almost the beginning, the company needed another to help deal with the company's growing number of licenses and classifications.

At the same time, a young designer from Connecticut was looking for a job.

Kelly Rector came from a world of privilege. Her mother, Gloria Kelly, was a former model who appeared in *Vogue* magazine, and her father, Tully Rector, was a well-known director of commercials. Kelly and her sister Amy had the privilege of growing up in the affluent enclave of Westport, Connecticut, a preppy haven on the Long Island Sound which would later become home-guru Martha Stewart's base of operations.

The Rector girls were athletic and spent much of their time swimming, playing with their dogs, or riding horses, which for Kelly meant a jumper named Fur Balloon.

"The second I sat on a horse, I just wanted to ride horses forever," Rector said.

Even as a child, Kelly had an affinity for fashion, as she "was one of those people able to put clothes together and look terrific," Tully Rector said.

All of this picture-book perfection came to a crash in Kelly's preteen years. Tully Rector had fallen in love with another woman, leaving Gloria to deal with the aftermath. Her parents divorce changed the financial picture of the family considerably, and Kelly's beloved Fur Balloon had to be sold.

Gloria Kelly remarried soon thereafter, and the new family—her daughters, her new husband, and his family—moved into a town house on New York's Upper East Side. In the ensuing years, Kelly's focus shifted from horses, a logistical challenge in the city, to fashion. Though this marriage was not destined to last more than a couple of years, Kelly Rector was in her element in New York City and stayed, though her mother eventually left for California.

A natural beauty with glossy brown hair, glowing skin, and striking sea-blue eyes, Kelly attracted her share of men. She met her first long-term boyfriend, Sam Edelman, while she was still a teenager in high school. Edelman was the son of a wealthy shoe manufacturer—the licensee for Polo Ralph Lauren shoes, in fact—who would later become the Sam in Sam & Libby shoes. Their relationship lasted for more than five years, with Kelly becoming a de facto member of the Edelman clan, at times living at his parents' home in Connecticut. Though the romance didn't work out, the duo remained close friends, and Edelman helped Rector get her first job after graduating from the Fashion Institute of Technology in 1979.

Kelly started as a receptionist at Polo Ralph Lauren, which seemed a perfect fit for her classic, preppy style. She soon made her way from the front desk to the design studio as an assistant, but was not happy at the company. A real horse-woman, Kelly didn't seem to enjoy her place in authenticating Lauren's fictional world.

Though she had moved on romantically, Rector again turned to Edelman for career advice. Coincidently, Edelman had heard of a design position at Calvin Klein and called his friend, designer Jeffrey Banks, for advice.

"I got a call from Sam Edelman," Banks said. "He asked me if I could call Calvin about Kelly.

"I knew Kelly," Banks said, so it was no imposition. "She had taught me how to ride, and her sister Amy ended up working with me at Merona [a sportswear company Banks designed for]."

"I called Calvin and said 'there's this great lady, Kelly Rector, who is looking for a job,' " Banks said, playing her up. " 'You've got to see this girl. She's really great and you're going to fall in love with her.'

"I'll never forget saying that," he added, ". . . my famous last words," which he later discovered had come true when he ran into the couple a short time later. "I was at this restaurant called Texarkana one Sunday night, and I saw them in the back of the restaurant," Banks said, realizing they had forged a more personal relationship. "Calvin waved me over."

From the start, Klein was attracted to the young stylist and her Waspy all-American good looks that made her the perfect foil for Klein's designs. Though he was not immediately thrilled with hiring former Polo Ralph Lauren employees, there was something about Kelly that he liked. Besides her style of dressing, her looks, and her demeanor, the designer really latched onto the quality of her skin.

Around the office, Rector became known as "the skin girl," as Calvin, and eventually her fellow designers, would test potential colors for his designs by putting them against her complexion, which was on the tan side.

Not long after her arrival at the company, it became apparent that Klein and Rector were well suited for each other. They were inseparable friends, to the extent that the duo would double-date—Klein with model Lisa Taylor and Rector with whomever she was dating at the time.

Much to the chagrin of the rest of the design staff, Rector rose rapidly through the ranks as a result of her personal relationship with Klein. She had the ear of Klein as a most trusted assistant and an alter ego of the designer himself. As such, she helped to shape the image and products of the house.

This subtle shift in power did not sit well with longtime collaborator Zack Carr, whose position was being usurped by Rector. He had been with Calvin Klein since the early years of the company, and the two were stylistically in sync. "He was the fantasy to Calvin's gut," a source close to the company said. However, Carr's ability to anticipate exactly what Klein wanted no longer mattered. Rector had risen to become the one who made the decisions.

The conflict within the Rector-Carr-Klein triumvirate came to a head in the days and hours before Klein's 1984 fall fashion show. In the days leading up to a designer's fashion show, the staff works around the clock, fitting clothes, making subtle adjustments, and arranging and rearranging the lineup. Nerves are frayed and tempers are short, as there are millions of sales dollars and priceless editorial decisions riding on this 20-minute presentation. Klein's collection had been inspired by his girlfriend Kelly, and therefore she felt it appropriate to express her opinions, which were exactly the opposite of Carr's. Caught in the middle, Klein didn't choose, but instead stormed out.

The show went on as originally planned, until it was time for the curtain call, when the designer takes a stroll on the catwalk. Instead of Klein coming out alone, as is de rigueur, his six assistants, Carr and Rector included, took a bow. Klein had left the building.

Days later, Carr left the company in a postshow fit and signed a deal with Gruppo Finanziario Tessile (GFT), an Italian company that would eventually manufacture Calvin Klein's menswear, to create the Zack Carr Collection.

Rector won that round with Klein and was subsequently given the title of design director. At the same time, their personal relationship was intensifying before the eyes of their colleagues.

"When she spent the night, we knew," said a colleague. "She'd come in in the same clothes. It was like a press release in a funny way."

The so-called press release making its way through the office grapevine was that Klein and Rector were on the verge of getting married, though they coyly denied it. Rector, by design or coincidence, took the summer off to train with her horse, True Blue, for the Hampton Classic riding competition, thus avoiding the rumors altogether.

However, she was back in the saddle later that month when she accompanied Klein and several members of the design staff on a fabric buying trip to Italy. On this trip, the duo impulsively married in Rome, with Rector wearing an off-white silk suit and lace blouse, "It's by Calvin, of course," and Klein, wearing a gray double-breasted wool suit.

"We decided to get married in Rome because we both love Italy so much and Kelly wanted to be married here," Klein said. "We were here for work and decided to marry before going back to New York."

Klein later put his feelings into words: "To have someone

love you and care about you is truly what life is all about. To be able to sustain that love and passion would be the goal of my life."

Fashionwise, Calvin Klein's first collection to be shown after their marriage showed a renewed vitality, while at the same time staying true to his clean, classic tenets. This was also the first collection after Zack Carr's departure, which proved to Klein doubters that he, not Carr, was the driving force behind the design direction.

Calvin and Kelly's honeymoon, however, did not last long. The dual role of wife and design collaborator was difficult to navigate politically with the other staff members, and they weren't sure how to handle her change in title. Kelly also found out the hard way that design director/girlfriend is a very different animal from a design director/wife. It was as though the kid gloves came off from Calvin's perspective, a lesson Kelly learned about from the pointed end of Calvin's jabs. By the end of 1986, Rector moved on to pursue other projects, namely, she took an editorial position at *House & Garden* magazine.

While Kelly was not in the office influencing decisions, her involvement with Klein affected more than just his personal life. His entire demeanor changed, taking him from an edgy man who was compulsively looking for what's next to a man who had reached a pinnacle—in part because he got the girl and was part of the post-AIDS-era in crowd.

Klein played the role of adoring husband with gusto. Though he had bought Rector a number of serious presents, including her horse True Blue, her wedding jewelry was a spur-of-the-moment purchase. Klein wanted to remedy the situation, and when the Duchess of Windsor's jewelry became available at auction, Klein went for it.

The designer paid some $1.4 million to purchase for his bride the late Wallis Warburg Simpson Windsor's double strand of pearls, earrings, and a pendant—a gift that was talked about across the world. However, it was the ring he bought from this auction that changed everything all the way down to the bottom line.

"I did buy Kelly a wedding band, but it was at the last second, and I ran into Cartier right before I was getting on a plane to go to Italy," he said. However, while he was paging through the Sotheby's catalog for the Duchess of Windsor's sale, Klein came across a ring he thought Rector would prefer. "I thought it was an absolutely beautiful ring. It was an eternity ring. In England, an eternity ring is before the engagement ring, and it means 'forever.' I thought 'My god, I've got the next name. I've got the whole idea for the next perfume. It all makes so much sense.' "

The company was working on its follow-up scent to Obsession, a runaway hit that was helping the cosmetics company rack up $100 million in sales annually. Robin Burns had rounded up the same team—"nose" Ann Gottlieb and International Flavors & Fragrances—to develop a floral scent with the hope of hitting the jackpot again. The new fragrance was a blend of white flowers—freesia, white lily, and muguet—combined with a base of narcissus and sandalwood.

The cultural atmosphere in the late 1980s, however, was considerably different from the atmosphere a mere five years before. The postdisco mania that characterized the go-go 1980s was halted dead in its tracks with the discovery of the AIDS virus, which affected everything from music to movies to fragrance and its advertising. *Fantasy* and *family* were the buzzwords being bandied about by marketers, and old-fashioned romance was back.

The discovery of the eternity ring, coupled with Klein's new life, gave Calvin Klein a perfect yarn to spin for his new fragrance. However, there is some discrepancy regarding who found the name. Klein took credit early on, but it was

Barry Schwartz who actually did the bidding at Sotheby's in Geneva, Switzerland. And Schwartz considers the name the best idea he ever had for the business.

Still, the fragrance Eternity, Rector's entry into Klein's life, and their relationship steered Calvin onto a more mainstream path. The American consumer could more closely identify with a designer who had a beautiful young wife than one who partied until the wee hours every night.

Following the same strategy that was used for the Obsession launch, Klein was going to hit the road, making a series of personal appearances to introduce the fragrance to customers.

However, the company wanted to tease consumers first. Burns devised a strategy with Saks Fifth Avenue where the department store would introduce Eternity in June 1988, selling the fragrance at only its Fifth Avenue location until September, at which time it would go into wide distribution—to some 700 doors. This tactic has since become commonplace in the beauty industry.

By the start of 1988, the media was obsessed with Klein, or rather, he made sure they were. Klein regularly made himself available to the press, either on the social circuit with trophy-wife Kelly on his arm or through the regular means, most often talking about his new life and fragrance.

"I think you can look at the fragrances and say they clearly have something to do with me at each moment in my life," Klein said.

In early May 1988, however, the Eternity press machine, which had seemed to be gaining momentum, ground to a halt, with Klein nowhere to be seen. His public relations staff at first insisted that he was simply on a holiday in the Caribbean, but the rumor mills on Seventh Avenue switched into overdrive, coming up with various scenarios much worse than the reality. Had Klein's Studio 54 days finally caught up with the designer? Was he mortally ill? Receiving treatment in some undisclosed location?

Finally, the Klein camp was compelled to make a statement. "A little less than two weeks ago, I checked myself into Hazelden Foundation in Center City, Minnesota, for treatment," for alcohol and prescription drug abuse, Klein said. "I imagine that for almost anyone going through something like this it would be a private matter. In my situation, I feel compelled to make this public statement because of the many friends and colleagues who have supported my work over the years."

The cat was out of the bag, and Klein was facing up to all that he had been running from in the past. However, he bought into the program and all that it entailed. "I'm in the first year of my second life," he said. "I feel reborn. I really am seeing things differently."

The show went on once Klein emerged from rehab—to not unexpectedly dazzling results. Surprisingly, the designer and those around him dealt with the issue of Klein's problems up front, even keeping a sense of humor about it. "I hope that it does for Eternity what Elizabeth Taylor in the Betty Ford Clinic did for Passion," Robin Burns said, noting that Passion was the best-selling fragrance in America at the time.

Following the typical Calvin Klein road map, there was an extensive advertising campaign to support the launch of the brand. Instead of the edgy Jose Borain, Christy Turlington, Klein's new all-American girl, a warmer, friendlier signature model, was chosen to star in the Eternity campaign with French actor Lambert Wilson.

"I'm thinking I'm in love, and I'm thinking about Obsession and what Obsession represents," Klein said. "That kind of advertising is the exact opposite of what I want to do now. I want something completely different, something softer, something much more romantic, much subtler."

The television commercials, directed by Richard Avedon, depicted the couple in a warm, sunny locale being affectionate. In the Klein tradition, there was a provocative script.

"Would you still love me if I were a woman," Lambert asked Turlington.

"Forever, if I could always be your man," she replied.

The print campaign, shot in a sunny black and white by Bruce Weber, featured the couple playing with their children on the beach. It depicted the idyllic family, complete with baby, as seen by Klein. It was quite a leap to believe that the nudity of the Obsession ads begat this sort of lifestyle.

Interestingly, Klein's idyllic family at the office was being reassembled. Kelly had returned to the fold as vice president of special projects, and Zack Carr closed his namesake collection to come back to where he started. However this time around, the two former adversaries aligned themselves as allies against the mercurial Klein.

"What happened is that they just bonded over their relationship with Calvin," a source close to the company said. "I think Kelly became a muse for Zack, ultimately, as so many other girls that passed through that place did."

Zack and Kelly became "fast friends, collaborators and colleagues," said Paul Wilmot, helping to cement Klein's position as the leading American designer. "This was the moment when the Calvin Klein collection became the most highly respected line of ready-to-wear in America enjoying rave reviews and eclipsing the competition in sales volume. . . . Zack was the galvanizing force," he added.

CHAPTER **8**

Unraveling

In contrast to the successes the design house was experiencing with underwear and fragrances, Calvin Klein jeans were dead on arrival by 1985, as was the rest of the designer jeans market. The denim cycle had peaked in the early 1980s, leaving manufacturers with dwindling sales and dried-up profits. Sadly, Klein was in a worse position than many of his designer jeans rivals: Because of his company's ambitious purchase of Puritan, Calvin Klein was not just a licensor with no royalties, *it was the manufacturer.* What's worse, Calvin Klein and Barry Schwartz were on the hook to Manufacturers Hanover Trust, the bank that loaned the company the more than $75 million to buy Puritan in the first place.

With no potential revenue on the horizon to offset the enormous payments that the partners would have to start making, they looked for long-term alternatives to pay the company's short-term debt.

Barry Diller was a friend of Klein's from the Studio 54

days, when Diller and his consort, designer Diane von Furstenberg, traveled in the same celebrity-filled crowd Klein did. The entertainment guru was quickly approaching mogul status as chairman of Paramount Pictures in 1985, and he was becoming a trusted business adviser to Klein and Schwartz.

Diller did business with Drexel Burnham Lambert and recommended the duo do the same. Michael Milken, the chief of Drexel's junk-bond division, was quickly gaining a reputation as a wizard who was able to create financing where none existed before by selling debt, or junk, for repayment later at high interest rates.

In the fall of 1985, Klein and Schwartz attended a Drexel High Yield Bond Conference, famously referred to as a "Predators' Ball," that led to smashing results—a $70 million injection of cash.

Required filings with the Securities and Exchange Commission (SEC) revealed that Drexel sold $45 million in eight-year notes that carried a 13⅞ percent interest rate. It also sold $25 million in 10-year notes that carried a rate of 14⅝ percent. Both offerings allowed the borrowers to pay only interest for the first five years, giving Schwartz and Klein breathing room in which to straighten out their business.

Buyers of Calvin Klein junk bonds included CenTrust Savings Bank, a now-defunct Miami savings and loan; Bass Investment Limited Partnership; Elid Inc., a Los Angeles holding company; Executive Life Insurance; and Great American Life Insurance. Milken's Drexel also got a nice piece for facilitating the financing.

"The pressures of meeting the obligations that we incurred at Puritan were pretty great," Schwartz said at the time, adding that the Manufacturers Hanover loans were more than the company could handle. "This is a chance for us to breathe, to consolidate our company and grow."

Unfortunately for Klein and Schwartz, this float of the company's debt put the company in the proverbial fishbowl that public companies live in. Because the notes were able to be resold to other investors, the SEC required regular filings of the company's financial statements.

For instance, SEC documents showed that despite the company's income being down 20 percent in 1984, to $17.2 million, both Klein and Schwartz received a salary of $700,000 with dividends and other payments of $11.3 million.

While the company toyed with the idea of making an initial public offering, Drexel's valuation of the company was a disappointment to Klein and Schwartz, and they abandoned the idea.

Calvin Klein's menswear business was, for the most part, a success. Through the company's sweeping license with Bidermann, just about every category was covered and was a certified success, bringing in decent royalties. Klein's relationship with Maurice Bidermann, however, left something to be desired.

Besides Klein and Schwartz's natural distaste for a licensee making more money from their branded product than they did, the haughty Frenchman took liberties beyond what Klein believed was appropriate, the most repugnant of which was signing rival designer Ralph Lauren to a women's licensing deal in the early 1980s.

Klein was already disenchanted by his dealings with Bidermann. He personally disliked the man and, once again, believed there was more money to be made with another menswear licensee or by manufacturing the collection in-house. Klein chose to distance himself from Bidermann by delegating design responsibilities to minions, and Bidermann took this chance to scale down the quality of the products, at first in subtle ways, with materials or trims used. However, it got to the point where design decisions were being made without Klein's input at all, or if he was asked for cursory approval, it was too late to facilitate any changes. The licensor with legendary control had finally lost it—the Bidermann license was a runaway train.

In 1986, Calvin Klein, Inc., filed what would be the first lawsuit in its history where the objective was to get out of its license deal. However, it would not be the last. Klein charged that Bidermann was using poor-quality materials. Bidermann countersued, claiming that Klein was interfering with business, and the impasse went to arbitration. Klein and Schwartz paid dearly to extract the company from this deal—an immediate $11.4 million in cash and an additional $2.2 million—at a time when cash counted. The royalty stream from menswear, however tainted, was revenue the company desperately needed.

"We bought back the men's wear license because it hampered us," Schwartz said. Klein clarified that the company intended to make higher-priced men's clothing collections, something Bidermann refused to do.

However, it would be over five years before the company entertained the notion of doing menswear again.

Calvin Klein's menswear license was not the only area causing Klein and Schwartz trouble. The duo's relationship with Minnetonka's Robert Taylor never really improved after its first ugly steps. However, the ambassador's role played by Robin Burns and the unprecedented successes they were experiencing with Obsession and Eternity made whatever dealings they had with Taylor much easier to take.

As was proving to almost always be the case, Klein and

Schwartz, though making a fortune from the license with Minnetonka, wanted more. Already owners of 30,000 Minnetonka shares they received in the sale of Calvin Klein Cosmetics, the duo from the Bronx bought shares of the company on the open market as a way of manipulating Taylor from afar.

By March 1986, Klein and Schwartz added enough to file a statement of ownership with the SEC, stating that they owned 6.7 percent of the company's outstanding shares, alerting Taylor to their actions.

Meanwhile, Minnetonka was trying to evolve from a dowdy soap company to a leader in fragrance and beauty by concentrating on its department store brands—Calvin Klein in particular, sales of which accounted for more than half the company's earnings in 1986. The company started moving in that direction by selling its Softsoap brand to Colgate-Palmolive in 1987.

The duo continued gradually accumulating Minnetonka stock, making a filing when they hit 9.2 percent ownership and then again when they hit 12.7 percent at the end of 1987. At that time, though, the company issued a press release assuring investors that the purchase was made for investment purposes. However, Klein and Schwartz also said they and others "at some point may determine to seek control of Minnetonka."

In what was seen as a strictly defensive move, Minnetonka created a stock ownership plan for employees, issuing 2.3 million new shares for $30 million. This amount was equivalent to the number of shares held by Schwartz, Klein, and their company, putting them on equal footing in the event of a fight.

Whether it was the so-called poison pill provision or the dwindling financial resources of Calvin Klein, Klein and Schwartz backed down from challenging Minnetonka's

Taylor. Perhaps they learned from the disastrous experience of buying Puritan, but chances are, the partners realized they wouldn't be able to raise the money to buy Minnetonka.

Robert Taylor, however, had had enough. In early 1989, he hired investment banker Morgan Stanley to explore the option of selling Minnetonka and its brands. Unilever NV emerged as the winner of a bidding war with five other companies, offering to pay $22.86 a share, or $376.2 million, for the company. Unilever was interested only in the Calvin Klein portions of the business and negotiated to sell off the company's other divisions as it took possession of the company.

Klein and Schwartz emerged as the winners in this transaction. Not only did they avoid a costly battle to buy Minnetonka, but their licensing revenue stream remained intact, they no longer had to deal with Robert Taylor, and they were paid $50.3 million for their holdings in Minnetonka, money that CKI was beginning to need desperately.

The end of the 1980s brought about sobering realizations for many businesses. The stock market, hit with a steep drop in 1987, hadn't quite recovered, and the country plunged into a recession accompanied by high unemployment.

Calvin Klein, Inc., was definitely feeling the crunch: it had no menswear business, sales of jeans were in the dumper, and the company was feuding with the owner of its fragrance business. While the high-end women's collection business was a bright spot, it wasn't remotely big enough to offset the losses being experienced elsewhere. Consequently, CKI's bottom line was lagging. The company reported a loss of $4.3 million in 1990, the third time the company had been in the red in the past five years.

What's worse, payment of principal on the bonds started

in 1990 and almost tapped out the company's available cash by the next year. And that was only the beginning—the company had an additional $55 million to pay back in the coming years. In 1991, the company said that if it couldn't generate the cash to make the payments, it "may use alternatives or additional sources of financing," perhaps taking on private equity investors, for instance. The situation looked dire.

However, Calvin Klein's friends stood by their man.

Like Barry Diller before him, longtime friend David Geffen came up with a solution that would help his friends in their time of financial crisis—he bought the company's outstanding bonds.

Geffen paid in the range of $31 to $43 million to buy all of the company's outstanding debt, primarily from Altus, a division of Credit Lyonnais. Altus was run by former Drexel Burnham Lambert junk-bond guru Leon Black, who actually made a bid to convert the bonds to equity in Calvin Klein, Inc. The bonds had an outstanding face value of $62 million at maturity.

A recording industry mogul who started in the mailroom at William Morris, Geffen had worked as an agent and a talent scout for a number of record companies before founding Geffen Records. In 1990, Geffen sold his company, Geffen Records, to MCA for an estimated $550 million in stock. Seven months later, MCA was bought by Matsushita, transforming Geffen's stock into approximately $700 million in cash, making him a billionaire in the process.

To Geffen, spending the millions to buy the bonds of Calvin Klein, Inc., was a drop in the bucket. But to his friends Klein and Schwartz, the gesture meant the world and saved the company.

"David went into the market and bought $55 million worth of bonds and said to us, get your house in order,"

Schwartz said. "I'll sit on this and you don't have to worry about paying this back. . . . When you can afford this, pay me back.

"People raised an eyebrow," Schwartz said, and asked, "what did David get out of this? David didn't get anything out of it. David did it as a friend."

And Geffen's admiration for his friend knew no bounds. "I believe Calvin is one of the smartest people I know and is a guy whose talent I not only believe in, but admire and respect," Geffen told *WWD*. "There is no downside for me," he said, adding, "Look . . . it doesn't represent 5 percent of my net worth."

Though he said at the time that he didn't want to be involved in the day-to-day operations, Geffen did lend a hand where he thought it appropriate. The renowned deal maker worked with Schwartz to restructure the company from one that manufactures to one that licenses its brand name.

Imagewise, Geffen made a suggestion that resulted in a deal that all of America was aware of—Calvin Klein signing rapper Marky Mark to model, and drop trou for the company's underwear advertisements.

The reversal of fortune that took place was swift, and with the economy again beginning to pick up, Klein took out a bank loan in 1993 to repay Geffen.

CHAPTER 9

What Is Calvin Klein?

Calvin Klein Inc.'s status as a 20-year-old business in the late 1980s was an anomaly in an industry where companies come and go with the trends. Its duration was a testament to its ability to evolve with the times under the direction of Calvin Klein.

"He understands the zeitgeist, and he's been able to do things that have played into what will be the mood in the future," said a former exec. "One can think of a number of instances where his business has thrived because he's launched a product at just the right moment," particularly jeans and Obsession.

However, the company's success was all-dependent on whether Klein was present. And in this time period, he was distracted. He was struggling with his postrehab sobriety, the company was extinguishing financial fires quarterly, Puritan Fashions' operations were still being integrated into the company, and the company's fashion direction was suffering as a result of it.

Was Calvin Klein a jeans company? Recent sales didn't say so. Was it a fragrance company and underwear company? Was it a sportswear company? If so, Calvin Klein Sport needed an overhaul. Was it a high-end designer brand? Sales of its lower-priced offerings like underwear and fragrance products suggested otherwise. The brand and company was at a crossroads it had to pass through in order to survive and continue to thrive.

At this time, there was a movement with fashion designers opening their own stores. Department and specialty stores were fine for selling the product, but they would never give designers the space to show their collections to the extent they wanted to. Namesake stores, boutiques, allowed designers to show an entire collection in an environment they created. It was brand building and, to some degree, a form of advertising that harkens back to the ateliers of the haute couture. Giorgio Armani had a sleek, modern space on New York's Madison Avenue, and Gianni Versace operated an over-the-top outpost on Fifth Avenue.

Ralph Lauren's Polo store in the Rhinelander Mansion on New York's Madison Avenue was the perfect example of a designer's retail space projecting his image. The rooms of the mansion were merchandised to look as if you'd stepped into the estate of your wealthy great aunt, complete with stuffy portraits of the ancestors. This was the kind of thing Calvin Klein wanted for himself.

The designer's first store opened in Dallas in 1988 though a partnership with a local society couple who were fans of the designer. It was the first in what the designer hoped would be a chain of retail expansion into cities that didn't have major stores carrying Calvin Klein merchandise.

The Dallas store was a testament to architecture, but the clothes didn't sell.

"You could see the white leather and you could see the mission furniture, but you couldn't see clothes," recalled Marty Staff, then the director of retail for Calvin Klein.

"Calvin loved the store, but it did not do business. I recommended that Calvin and Barry buy it, so we bought that store and modified it and business got somewhat better."

The experience whet the designer's appetite for more. "Calvin wanted to open other stores," Staff said. "He was reawakening," absorbing new knowledge "like a sponge."

Calvin Klein stores in Palm Beach and Boston soon followed, and in each case, Klein immersed himself in learning about the process.

"We had a ritual where we would meet every Saturday in the store," in Palm Beach, Staff recalled. At that time, Calvin and Kelly would spend winter weekends in the south so she could ride her horses.

"We would drive around and look at malls . . . at stores," Staff continued. "He honestly didn't know why his merchandise was in a certain part of the store. He didn't understand the difference between moderate and better, and what those different gradations were in the store, because he was disconnected—he hadn't been in stores.

"He later became an expert, beyond anything I knew. He just sort of absorbed the whole thing. And I just think it's at that point that he also realized that he had some issues— quality issues, distribution issues, and product issues."

Armed with his newfound knowledge, Klein examined the divisions of the company, with his gaze falling on the Puritan division, which had been renamed Calvin Klein Sport and produced Calvin Klein Sport for men and women, Calvin casual sportswear, and Calvin Klein men's underwear.

This division was operating without a raison d'être—it was too fragmented—and though the jeans business was

starting to show signs of life again, the sportswear was simply unhip.

"Calvin and Barry bought the jeans company, but they
didn't really know what to do with it," Staff said. "One of
Calvin's first big decisions, a famous one, was to take the
name off the jeans, which gave the consumer absolutely no
reason to buy it. When they did that, business just tanked."

At that time, the department store business in American
was evolving. Women's moderately priced classification de-
partments that sold suits, dresses, and coats were becoming
more integrated by brand, where classifications were mixed
to represent looks from a manufacturer or designer.

The gap between high-priced designer offerings and
more moderately priced sportswear was growing. Companies were creating something that would bridge that gap,
falling in the middle pricewise and also stylewise. The
"bridge" category was created, and companies like Anne
Klein, Ellen Tracy, and Donna Karan merchandised collections for this area.

"When Donna Karan diffused her line and created DKNY,
it became a backbone bridge resource," Staff said. Klein
wanted the same for his lower-priced collection, but he
couldn't take the moderate Calvin Klein Sport and move it
up, so something new had to be created.

"He wanted it to be more sophisticated and better quality
and more modern," Staff clarified. It was a chance for Klein
to start over. The seeds of what would become the cK collection had been planted.

But first, the company had to get its menswear on the mend.
When Klein and Schwartz extracted themselves from the
Bidermann licensing agreements for menswear, their idea

was always to relaunch a men's collection that was wholly owned by Calvin Klein, like the women's collection. However, the company's precarious financial position dictated that any start-up be put on hold, unless it could be pushed through existing channels. The only things Calvin Klein was selling to men in the late 1980s and early 1990s were underwear and jeans, manufactured by the Calvin Klein Sport division, and fragrances through Unilever.

It was a situation Klein desperately wanted to remedy. At the same time, there was an Italian-tailored clothing maker that was looking for new, younger designers to rev up its branded business.

Gruppo Finanziario Tessile (GFT) was an established Italian suit manufacturer of the old order. The company, a division of the late Giovanni Agnelli's Holding di Participazioni Industriali (HdP), was vertically integrated from fabric mill to manufacture, and it held the licenses for European designers like Giorgio Armani, Ungaro, Claude Montana, and Valentino. However, the designers in its stable were established, with businesses that had hit plateaus. GFT was in search of new blood.

The company's search turned to the United States and the designers who were perceived to be on the fast track—Donna Karan, Ralph Lauren, and Calvin Klein.

"My proposal was that we go with full steam ahead with one major American designer," said former GFT marketing vice president Pablo de Echevarria. Klein was the company's choice.

"The main reason we decided to go with Calvin was that he was somebody who had his fingers on the pulse not only of America," he said, but potentially the world.

The negotiations with Klein, Schwartz, and the GFT executives were "long and drawn," a former insider said, but by

July 1991, a deal was in place for GFT to manufacture and distribute Calvin Klein's men's collection, the more expensive line, and a diffusion collection.

However, GFT didn't realize what it was getting itself into with that deal.

"Calvin sees the licensing contract as the floor of the negotiating process to get more and more," the insider said. "And it doesn't matter how much you give—Calvin always wants more. That's the joke among the licensees. What does Calvin want? Calvin wants more."

Luckily, the Calvin Klein collection, manufactured by GFT, took off immediately from the time it hit the stores in fall 1992.

With men's buttoned up, Klein and Schwartz turned their attention to the company's jeans division. The fashion pendulum had swung back, and sales of jeans were picking up. This time around, though, there were more options for treating the fabrics—stone washes, acid washes, and enzyme washes. Consequently, denim was being used in its many iterations and weights for items other than jeans: Shirts, skirts, dresses, and jackets were being made in the durable fabric, and the offerings from Calvin Klein Jeans grew into an actual sportswear collection.

However, the designer had to compete in an arena that was much more crowded that it had been the previous time around. A denim-driven sportswear company named Guess had picked up where Klein left off, making sexy, jeans-filled advertising campaigns its standard. European companies like Marithé and François Girbaud, Rifle, Chevignon, and Diesel also burst onto the scene, offering new finishes for denim with a European flair. To put the company back on the map, Klein would have to make a bold statement.

The answer was a 116-page advertising supplement, produced by Klein's in-house ad agency CRK, that would chronicle the activities of an imaginary rock band on tour.

The "outsert" featured an extensive cast of characters, including model Carre Otis and future male supermodel Marcus Schenkenberg, in a series of provocative images shot by Bruce Weber. Naked women, in the midst of sexual acts with denim-clad rockers, were sprinkled through the supplement. What really got engines revving were the shower shots of Schenkenberg wearing nothing but a pair of jeans strategically draped over his privates. It cost the company $1 million to poly-bag 250,000 copies of the outsert with *Vanity Fair*'s October 1991 issue; it was received by subscribers and could be bought on newsstands in New York and Los Angeles.

"He wanted to do something disruptive to catch people's attention," said mouthpiece Paul Wilmot.

Catch people's attention he did. Klein supported the piece with an all-jeans fashion show that featured biker babes, raunchy music by Prince, and bare breasts, as well as a $10 million jeans advertising campaign.

Bloomingdale's reported that Calvin Klein jeans sales jumped 30 percent in the weeks following the release of the supplement.

"I always try to make a statement and this campaign with the motorcycles . . . looking very free, young and sexy, the rock-and-roll, is doing just what I hoped it would," Klein told *WWD*.

Calvin Klein was leading the pop culture again with his sexy, provocative imagery. Sex seemed to be the trend everyone was embracing, from Claudia Schiffer in the Guess ads to the fashion-and-sex obsessed videos of performer George Michael. Madonna, cut from the same reinventive cloth as the designer, did Calvin one better with her *Sex* book, a collaboration with Steven Meisel and editor Glenn O'Brien that was released in 1992.

However cutting-edge the outsert was, in the end it didn't quite do the job. Six months after the campaign hit, sales weren't any more affected than the immediate initial boost. Federated Department Stores, parent to Bloomingdale's and Macy's, reported there wasn't "any noticeable impact in sales."

"That was the old thinking," de Echevarria said of the supplement. "It was okay, but it was still a little bit cheesy. It convinced the existing base of Calvin customers," but it didn't speak to the younger customers Klein needed.

It was time for the image maker to go back to the drawing board.

There are two common denominators in Calvin Klein's advertising portfolio—sex and the ability to anticipate what the next big thing will be. Within those areas, Klein was challenged to walk the tightrope between being sexy and being vulgar, between knowing what was going to appeal to consumers and what would repulse them.

The designer has an innate sense of what is right for the moment and what's going to push people's buttons. More important, he understands that he is only as good as the people he surrounds himself with.

"Calvin's extremely innovative," said an inside source. "He's surrounded himself with amazing people that allow him to stay in the position that he's been in. It is a talent for Calvin to be able to recognize those people and pay for them to be around."

Photographers, clothing stylists, hair stylists, makeup artists, and creative directors would come and go throughout the history of the company, each leaving their indelible mark on the campaigns they worked on.

While the company was being overhauled stylewise, its advertising was also being reexamined. The most consistent images the company put out were those for its fragrances Obsession and Eternity, particularly for print advertising.

Obsession had grown to include men's and women's fragrances, body products, and shampoo. Each of these classifications had its own separate set of images, yet side by side they looked like they came from the same sexy, skin-baring portfolio.

Eternity's frolicking family came across with warm feelings from model Christy Turlington, though the man of the family changed several times, as did the children. Consumers continued to buy into Turlington's rose-colored life regardless of how many different model "husbands" she had, and they continue to do so today.

In 1990, the company had experimented with a new television campaign for Obsession. Klein hired film director David Lynch to take the surrealism of the first Obsession campaign ("Ah, the smell of it") one step further. Lynch, known for his offbeat movie *Blue Velvet,* was enjoying small-screen success for his wacky and disturbing television series *Twin Peaks.*

The new campaign featured actors, many from *Twin Peaks,* reciting lines from the classics that dealt with obsession. Passages from *The Great Gatsby, The Sun Also Rises, Madame Bovary,* and *Women in Love* were recited by actors Benicio Del Toro, Heather Graham, Lara Flynn Boyle, and James Marshall. It was touted as a return to romance.

While the creative was being tested and changed, those who created were also changing.

Sam Shahid, Calvin Klein's longtime creative director for all advertising, left CRK advertising to head up Banana Republic's efforts, taking several key staffers with him. Advertising exec Tonne Goodman left Calvin to become fashion director at *Harper's Bazaar,* and Paul Wilmot, Klein's longtime publicity man, left to join *Vogue.*

There were many hired to fill the voids these departures created, with Neil Kraft coming on board to head up KRT and Fabien Baron stepping in as the company's creative director for imaging.

Modelwise, the company had moved beyond using only Jose Borain. Turlington was under an exclusive contract for advertising, but was used primarily for fragrance. There wasn't just one signature Calvin Klein model—the company was experimenting with many models. In fact, in 1992, Klein featured a model he had regularly used in the 1970s, Lisa Taylor, in a campaign for the high-end collection.

The 40-year-old model was an anomaly at the time, as models over the age of 25 were rarely seen. The campaign came about after several chance meetings.

"I actually ran into Calvin in New York at some screening," Taylor recalled. She called him when she returned to her home in Los Angeles and suggested he do a campaign featuring older models.

"He was already thinking about it. Older women *were* the people who were buying his couture stuff."

Klein and photographer Steven Meisel were also discussing a concept that reflected Klein's real women. "It was timing—it all came together and we did it," Taylor concluded.

"I'm not into this one woman represents what I do," Klein told *WWD.* "That's a little old-fashioned."

Interestingly, all it took for Klein to change his mind was a skinny English teenager.

The larger-than-life supermodel craze was winding down in the early 1990s with Linda Evangelista, Naomi Campbell, Christy Turlington, and Cindy Crawford suffering from over-exposure. Their over-the-top existence and the sound bites that accompanied them ("I won't get out of bed for less than $10,000 a day") symbolized the 1980s greed-is-good mentality. The country, in a recession, was less and less receptive to this concept, particularly as fashions were moving toward a street vibe, with grunge and hip-hop coloring the runways.

The phrase "kinder and gentler" was in constant use, but it truly did come to symbolize what was happening with fashion models at the time. Smaller women were being considered for runways and ad campaigns in a world where the norm used to be "bigger is better." Shorter, more petite models with gamine looks reminiscent of the English girls of the 1960s started cropping up editorially and in ad campaigns; they even made appearances on the catwalk, usually the domain of Amazon-like women.

Kate Moss, at five feet six inches, was at the forefront of this movement. At 18, she still looked like the 14-year-old who was discovered in the airport while traveling home from holiday. She quickly became a favorite with photographers Steven Meisel, Bruce Weber, and Mario Sorrenti, who became her boyfriend.

Creative director Fabien Baron used Moss for a shoot in *Harper's Bazaar* and brought her to Klein's attention. The designer quickly snatched up Moss for his own use, signing her to a contract and making her his new signature model.

Moss's entry into Klein's life changed the whole picture, literally.

The original Obsession ads, with the naked limbs akimbo, needed to be replaced. While the images were certainly timeless, Klein had moved beyond what they represented. In Moss, Klein found a new muse, a perfect woman, and an obsession, as it were. Her boyfriend, photographer Mario Sorrenti, felt the same way. Klein took the unorthodox step of sending Moss and Sorrenti on location to an obscure

Caribbean island alone with the instructions to come back with a new Obsession campaign.

The new images were clearly of a woman who is loved by the camera and by the man operating it. Sorrenti showed Moss in a series of grainy black-and-white images. She is naked in almost all of them, exposing her clearly underdeveloped body to the camera in a way that her expression is conveying knowledge, trust, and also the spirit of someone who is being hunted.

Investor David Geffen's official entrance into the house of Klein was touted as a token of friendship. He repeatedly told the press he didn't want to meddle in the company's operations, though with his track record of building bands into multi-million-dollar brands, he clearly could help. Instead, he insisted he was buying his friends an opportunity to regroup and reposition.

Geffen may have been trying all along to make suggestions to Klein about his imagery or choice of models, but didn't feel it was his place. His investment, coupled with the arrival of one muscle-bound trou-dropping kid from the streets of Boston on the pop music scene, spurred him on to make a suggestion that resulted in the most successful partnership of artist and designer in the history of fashion.

Mark Wahlberg was the younger brother of former New Kids on the Block band member Donnie Wahlberg. Too young and too rough to be included in that band, Mark had musical aspirations of his own and, in 1991, hit it big with a rap-dance song called "Good Vibrations."

The performer, with his broad, muscular shoulders and six-pack stomach, attracted huge crowds to each of his performances in dance clubs and concerts. But they were not just coming for the music—Marky Mark's gimmick was that he would drop his already low-slung jeans during the performance, revealing his boxer-brief-clad derriere. It drove crowds wild, whether gay or straight, and created a look that younger consumers would make their own, allowing their jeans to fall below the waistband of their underwear.

Geffen brought Marky Mark to Calvin Klein, urging the designer to use the young performer in his advertisements. In Marky Mark, Klein found a vehicle that would bring the company to a new level. It wasn't just a jeans, fragrance, or fashion company—Calvin Klein, and its underwear, had become iconic—more a pop culture touchstone than it ever was before.

"Marky's involvement was such a natural progression for me," Klein said. "He is the quintessential symbol of the young hip crowd to whom the clothing appeals. He's the best."

The rapper graced Klein's print advertisements topless, in only underwear and jeans. The boyish man was also joined in many of the ads by Kate Moss. The combination was a sexual powder keg, particularly when she is also shown topless. Wahlberg could look boyish, sexy, and slightly bad (in a good way) all at the same time, while Moss projected an all-knowing innocence. The images were unbeatable in terms of appealing to a younger consumer, which was confirmed the day the ads hit the street.

"The first place we debuted that campaign was in LA," said a former insider. "It was in bus shelters and phone booths. By five or six o'clock, we got a call to tell us 16 phone booths had already been vandalized for the posters," an indicator that was becoming a signature for Calvin Klein ads.

Klein followed up with a television campaign that carried the message even further. Though scripts were written for the Herb Ritts–directed commercials, once the rapper and

Moss were on set, Mark wanted to say things that were more natural for him. The resulting almost stream-of-conscious rambling worked on many different levels.

"Shouts go out to my man, Calvin Klein. Good looking out for the drawers," Wahlberg said, as Moss coyly paced around him. "Not saying I'm going to do another Fruit of the Loom commercial or nothing like that 'cause they don't make the hype shorts. These are the Nineties, man. They just fit good and they hold me snug, so if I'm about to go out and get some skins, I'm not about to put on no silk underwear. Ooh, she got freckles. . . . Now the best protection against AIDS is to keep your Calvins on."

He added, "Now that could definitely come between me and my Calvins," gesturing to Moss. "Do you have Calvin Klein underwear on?"

The foundation had been laid for Calvin Klein to know exactly what he needed to do—create a collection of less expensive, hip clothes that a younger consumer could wear. Beyond jeans, this collection would fit into the bridge area of department stores, giving the Klein brand an additional presence for consumers.

Klein recalled the genesis for cK came from a dinner he had with his twenty-something daughter, Marci, a television producer. "One night, we had dinner and she said, 'you know, Dad, I can't wear the clothes that you make. It's simply not appropriate for me to be spending that kind of money or dressing that way, coming to work at NBC. There are so many people like me. Why don't you make clothes for us?' "

Through a series of fits and starts, the sportswear collection known as cK finally hit its stride in fall of 1993.

Socially, Generation X was becoming the favored demographic. This was the first generation that did not expect to do better financially than the generation it followed. And this generation, children of baby boomers, was looking for something else—a different kind of job, new music, or just a good cup of coffee—and it had to be real.

Klein created cK with this demographic in mind and, to prove his point, proposed a fashion show featuring these real people—tattoos, dreadlocks, and all.

Fall of 1993 was the first time New York's fashion week had a central base of operations. The Council of Fashion Designers of America (CFDA) had erected tents in New York's Bryant Park to host the week of runway shows, and Calvin Klein's cK show was held on its first day.

According to an inside source, "The initial idea was to show all of these different clothes on a mix of real people and models," some 190 in total. This was one of the first times real people would be used by a fashion company on the runway to prove a point, and cK "was supposed to be for everybody."

"Models" were recruited in every way possible. Flyers were passed out, friends and friends of friends were called, strangers were approached on the street, and Klein even recruited models while he was working out at the David Barton gym.

"The Nineties are about real people and personal expression," Klein clarified, "people with an attitude who want clothing that represents their own personality and sense of style. It's what the public identifies with today."

The result was a stunning production played to a house filled beyond its 1,100-person capacity.

The show started with a video history of the designer's advertising stretching from before the days of Brooke Shields to Kate Moss and Marky Mark's flirtatious ads. And then the parade of people started down the catwalk one by one, each more interesting than the previous. It wasn't the clothing that made them interesting—clothing was something more basic, simple, and minimal—it was how they'd been chosen and the attitude with which they carried themselves. It was original and real, and the fan-packed audience reveled in Klein's being able to pare down what people wanted, again.

"The newest cK women's things . . . may very well be his landmark collection," said Kal Ruttenstein, senior vice president of fashion direction at Bloomingdale's. "He has a new energy and a new spirit, personally, and in the way he's doing things."

His "new energy" had earlier allowed Klein to take the world of Calvin Klein on the road, traveling to Los Angeles to stage a similar show, complete with 350 real people, for an AIDS Project Los Angeles fund-raiser in June 1993. Klein's new involvement with philanthropic work, particularly for organizations that supported AIDS, came directly from David Geffen. The mogul was very active in the cause and urged the designer to join him, arguing that it was his duty to follow suit.

The APLA show was every bit as exciting as the New York fashion show, perhaps even more so, as Marky Mark graced the runway and Tina Turner performed.

The uniqueness of the moment was not lost on a source close to the company. "Marky Mark was truly at the crossroads. It was so genius. To see him at the Hollywood Bowl—that moment was a moment that that comes once in a lifetime."

Not only was Klein at the top of his game designwise, sales were bounding into healthy territory, and he was also being recognized by the fashion industry, having been cited as both Women's Wear Designer of the Year and Men's Wear Designer of the Year by the CFDA for his designs in 1993.

CHAPTER 10

Fast, Furious, and Forte

The success Calvin Klein was experiencing was a direct result of the designer's renewed involvement in his company. With that involvement came opportunities for new business, but first, he had to pay back an old friend's generosity.

By June 1993, Klein and partner Barry Schwartz were in a position to pay David Geffen back for bailing out the company. Using the company's licensing income as collateral, the duo from Mosholu Parkway borrowed $58 million from Citibank at 6 percent interest, cutting the interest costs on the bonds (previously at 13⅞ and 14⅝ percent) in half.

While Geffen was no longer an investor in the company, Klein said Geffen would remain one of the company's trusted advisers. "He's one of the smartest and most creative businessmen I know," Klein said.

The company's turned-around financial status set the partners free to concentrate on business at hand—growing Calvin Klein through a series of deals that came at a fast and furious pace and would transform the company in positive, and profitable, ways.

Linda Wachner was an anomaly in the apparel industry.

As CEO and chairman of the Warnaco Group, Inc., she was one of few women to run a Fortune 500 company. A native of New York City, Wachner was ambitious from the start, graduating from high school at age 16. She continued her education at the State University of New York at Buffalo, where she studied economics and business administration. She entered the workforce as a buyer of bras, girdles, and women's apparel for Macy's and later ran Max Factor cosmetics before taking the helm of Warnaco in 1986 in a hostile takeover.

Once at Warnaco, the ball-busting blond turned the company's fortunes around, growing it from a nothing little bra-and-panty maker to a multibrand, multi-million-dollar company. Though her brash, hard-as-nails management style was legendary in apparel industry circles, her style was not much more aggressive than a male manager of her caliber. Still, her old-world, garmento way of operating inspired dislike from her subordinates and a wariness from those she did business with.

In 1994, her portfolio of brands included Warner's, Olga, Valentino *Intimo* intimate apparel, plus Hathaway and Chaps Ralph Lauren men's sportswear. However, she was missing a marquee brand. Wachner approached Klein and Schwartz over dinner in the Hamptons—she wanted to make Calvin Klein men's and women's underwear Warnaco's crown jewel brand.

A primary objective in a licensing deal is to partner with a company that is best in its field, the expert. As the owner of the brand, you know the product made by that expert will be top quality, in turn furthering the reach of your brand name. Klein and Schwartz recognized that Wachner and Warnaco were the best company in the industry to make their underwear and proceeded to negotiate.

The deal, finalized in February, included the purchase of the men's underwear business outright, the licenses for men's accessories worldwide, and women's innerwear when the company's current license with Heckler Manufacturing expired at the end of 1994. For these potentially valuable properties, Klein and Schwartz were paid $64 million plus ongoing fees and royalties.

For Warnaco, this acquisition would take the company to a whole new level of performance, with Wachner projecting men's sales could reach $300 million by 1997 from its current $70 million in annual sales. The women's business was expected to follow suit, reaching at least those levels.

This deal allowed the duo from the Bronx to emerge entirely debt-free, and it put Calvin Klein one step closer to being the design, marketing, and licensing company it was repositioning itself as. In this move to reposition, the duo finally conceded what their repeated mistakes over the years had proven to others—outside manufacturers could do a better job making and distributing Calvin Klein products than Calvin Klein could. It was an epiphany for the company that was to provide mixed results in the future.

Hot on the heels of the Warnaco deal, Klein and Schwartz were approached by a veteran apparel executive, Arnold Simon, with a deal they knew they shouldn't pass up—he wanted to buy Klein's jeans divisions.

Simon's company, Rio Sportswear Inc., was offering $35 million to acquire the Calvin Klein men's and women's jeans business and its assets, which included a laundry facility and a sewing plant. Rio would also be granted the licenses to manufacture and sell Calvin Klein jeans and jeans-related products from that point forward.

"Jeans started as a license, and now that we have our strategy to license out our business, it falls right into place," Klein told *WWD*.

However, the deal with Rio had one snafu—Rio itself was in play, with children's clothing maker OshKosh B'Gosh intending to buy the company.

Both deals were built on quicksand. Rio appeared to be having trouble with financing, and OshKosh, in its own financial doldrums, was hoping the Rio acquisition would establish it in the women's market. Also, OshKosh, which had originally agreed on the Calvin Klein acquisition, got cold feet and rescinded its support, causing a warning light to come on within Simon. "I didn't like the idea of doing business with people who didn't have the insight to see that Calvin could be a very big business," he said.

Not surprisingly, both deals fell apart, taking Klein and Schwartz back to square one. However, with their intentions to sell declared, other suitors—Lawrence Stroll's Pepe Jeans USA and Bill Farley's Fruit of the Loom—came calling.

Valued adviser David Geffen stepped in, throwing his vote to Fruit of the Loom based on the company's proposed aggressive spending on marketing and advertising. That tipped the scales in Fruit of the Loom's favor. By April 1994, Calvin Klein, Inc., agreed to sell its jeans division to Fruit of the Loom for close to $50 million plus future royalties.

But there was a problem with this deal—Farley wanted to broadly interpret the term "jeans-related products," giving him more leeway to manufacture items in related categories. Klein and Schwartz, sticklers for details, preferred a narrow interpretation, and this deal also unraveled.

The third time proved to be the charm in this denim

dance, and the winner was none other than Arnold Simon and Rio Sportswear. However, this time around, Simon brought in a financial partner, Charterhouse Group International, which allowed him to meet the $50 million asking price for the jeans division.

"I had a feeling the deal wasn't going to fly when I heard someone from [FTL] say that they intended to spin their own denim. Levi Strauss doesn't spin its own denim," Simon said.

At Calvin Klein, Inc., headquarters at 205 West 39th Street, these were the glory days. With business finally showing consistent and regular improvement, the mood around the offices was one of optimism. After Klein's stint in rehab and the subsequent turnaround of the company's financial status, he was operating from a base of confidence.

"Calvin was leading the company," said one former insider, and that leadership included hiring some of the best design talent available on Seventh Avenue.

Zack Carr was heading up the design staff, which included such names as Narciso Rodriguez, Stephen Fairchild, and John Varvatos, all of whom have their own successful collections today. Creative collaborations with hot photographers Joe McKenna, Steven Meisel, and Mario Sorrenti were all part of a day's work. Kelly Klein, Calvin's muse, was involved, contributing ideas on photography, which she eventually chose as her career. And then there was Carolyn Bessette.

Bessette gained national attention when she dated and subsequently married John F. Kennedy Jr. in 1996. The Greenwich, Connecticut–bred beauty had a cool, patrician Waspy look and a certain style of dressing that catapulted her from anonymity to the center of the universe at Calvin Klein.

Bessette started working for Klein in his Chestnut Hill store in Boston, but was quickly moved to the company's headquarters in New York to work in sales with private customers, mainly socialites. Obscurity was a short stop for Bessette, as she was noticed by several executives, including David Geffen.

"You have this gorgeous girl in the back closet," a source close to the company recounted, telling Klein, "I don't understand why she's not working for you in public relations." She quickly joined Lynn Tesoro and Rachel DiCarlo in the company's PR department, where she represented the company to the media and became another in-house muse for the designers.

"She wasn't telling people what to design," one former insider said, "but when Carolyn walked in, she would be stripped down—from her shoes to her sweaters to her skirts to who did her hair to her makeup," and the designers drank it in. "Carolyn was more an influence on Calvin than Kelly sometimes."

The women, particularly those who worked in public relations, even started to look like Bessette. With collection and cK the required dress code, "we all dressed alike and had the same hair color," said a naturally brunette former employee. "Carolyn gave me money to get my hair done," in dress-code blond. "She said, 'I don't care where you go, just tell me how much it is.' "

All of this homogeneity fit to create the image that is Calvin Klein. The brand was at its most pure in the company's offices. From the office's decor of concrete floors, white walls, and black furniture to the dress code of mainly black, gray, and white collection or cK clothes, the image was consistent.

Klein even "sent out a memo about the color of the paper clips you could use. "You could only use black [plastic] paper clips," recalled one former exec. "He sent out a memo that the trash cans had to be hidden." However, the exec added, "I learned from that—it was a consistent, a precise image."

And if you weren't following the precise guidelines, you undoubtedly were caught on one of the hundreds of fiber-optic surveillance cameras that were placed in every last nook and cranny of the building's 15 floors.

Barry Schwartz had been concerned with security from the very beginning, installing a series of surveillance cameras when the company had only a few floors at 205 West 39th Street and watching the monitors from his desk.

However, the extent of monitoring and security had grown beyond what seemed logical. By the early 1990s, Calvin Klein employed an armed staff of former New York City police officers in the offices at all times. These guards were charged with monitoring the wall of screens in what employees referred to as "Mission Control," to see what products were going where and who was doing what with whom.

One source suggested the excessive security was the result of an incident during a market week where someone broke into the offices and sprayed yellow paint on all the samples. Regardless, with hundreds of clothing samples being worked with daily (it can be concluded), these measures must have cut down on theft.

For Klein, a self-professed perfectionist, this was just the tip of the iceberg. Other edicts that came from him included such strange standards as allowing only white calla lilies in reception areas, only white orchids in offices, and no talking in the elevators. Personal items like photos or postcards were forbidden to grace your desk, and no eating was allowed at your desk. Klein's strict standards applied to his coffee as well. To ensure he'd get just the right mix of coffee and milk every time, there was a Pantone color swatch on the wall of the kitchen so that whoever was making it would get the ratio right.

Over the years, Klein and Schwartz outlined ambitious plans for expansion that included partnerships in Japan, selling collection and sportswear throughout Europe, opening stores in the United States and abroad, and finally, making Calvin Klein fragrances world brands. Though none of these aspirations seemed too far-fetched, Klein and Schwartz never seemed to have the engine or the structure behind the company to make it happen.

But the time was right for the duo to pursue more. They hired an executive search firm, Don Ross Associates, to find an executive who could run the company and take it to the next level of international expansion. One name repeatedly kept coming up—Giorgio Armani's Gabriella Forte.

There are still few designers with the international presence Giorgio Armani had in 1994. Through his multiple labels and price levels, which included Giorgio Armani, Armani Le Collezioni, Emporio Armani, and A/X Armani Exchange, the designer had created a fashion dynasty that made his products affordable to most at some level.

The designer's presence in the United States is credited to some very specific placements, most of which Forte was responsible for. Americans first became aware of Armani through the movie *American Gigolo,* in which star Richard Gere wears the designer's clothes, and a rainbow selection of Armani shirts are featured prominently in one scene.

Over the years, Forte, on behalf of Armani, courted celebrities like Jodie Foster, Annette Benning, Michelle Pfeiffer, and basketball coach Pat Reilly, dressing them for personal appearances and award shows. Combining the best of what she believed to be both worlds, Forte used her expertise in positioning and publicity and her mercurial temperament to build Armani into the powerhouse it was in 1994. To the world of fashion journalists, Forte *was* Armani.

However, in the world of Giorgio Armani, there is only one star, and that is Armani himself. Though the pint-sized, Italian-born, New York–bred Forte presided over Armani's international expansion and put him on the map across the world, there was a limit to what more she could achieve— more accurately, how far she could move up in the hierarchy. The opportunity to serve as president and chief operating officer at Calvin Klein, Inc., would put her on virtually equal footing with Klein and Schwartz.

Forte's departure from Armani shocked the fashion world, particularly since Armani was in the midst of some growing pains of its own. Simint SpA, the company that operated the A/X Armani Exchange business, needed an overhaul and was struggling financially, posting quarterly losses.

The Calvin Klein coup, however, was seen as a feather in the company's cap that would take it to the next level.

"Calvin is on a roll this year from a financial and credibility standpoint, and this is a real coup for him to steal away one of Armani's key people," Alan Millstein, a retail consultant, said at the time. However, he added, "She is walking into one of the hottest snake pits on Seventh Avenue."

Forte had nothing to fear at Calvin Klein. In her 15 years at Armani, she had earned the reputation as an unbelievably tough businesswoman who would go to any length to protect her designer. Nicknamed the "terrible terrier," the diminutive, long-haired brunette was a workaholic who slept less than three hours a night. And Klein, the perfectionist, had met his match in Forte, an obsessive perfectionist, who is so precise and observant, she notices when things on her desk have been moved in the slightest.

"Barry and I will be letting go of a number of things we've involved ourselves with, but our roles won't be diminished," Klein said. "When the company was smaller, I was involved in so many things. As the company grows and expands, you need a great management team."

Forte hit the ground running, establishing her presence in all areas of the company, expecting to take over all of the business dealings to leave Calvin Klein free to concentrate on his "process."

The first thing that changed was the company's operating hours. Fashion companies were known for their long hours, particularly in the periods just before fashion shows or during big photo campaigns. Forte, however, believed in the regular 20-hour workday.

"The office never closed," a source close to the company recalled. "You could work anytime—you never didn't work. And Calvin was totally engaged in the pace. He was very proud that you could get into the office at any hour of the night. That's how she worked."

Forte regularly held meetings after midnight, and the later they were, the more likely they were to be taped, so that the parties involved were reminded of what had been said the night before.

While Klein was a stickler for details, Forte was even more so. Staffers lived in fear of spot checks, where she would swoop into a department and reprimand them for dust, loose papers, or a messy desk.

"We were constantly using Fantastik and paper towels to wipe everything down," an ex-employee said.

The white calla lily/orchid rule was enforced even more strictly, with one of Forte's three assistants assigned the task of walking the floor after hours and leaving Post-it notes on the desks of offenders.

The dress code, which basically consisted of Calvin Klein

collection and cK pieces purchased with employee clothing allowance, got more and more strict with Forte's arrival. One incident in particular, caused her to react.

Forte was in an advertising meeting that included staffers on the executive level as well as some assistants. She noticed that one assistant in the room was wearing the same collection suit as she was. The next day a memo was issued stating that assistants were allowed to wear only cK in the office, not collection.

She took it a step further in the public relations office, actually issuing uniforms of a jacket, skirt, and trousers from collection to the women who worked there. They were required to wear a version of this combination every day.

More important, Forte established firm boundaries between levels of management where none had previously existed.

"Before her arrival, it was a little bit of a club or a family," said former exec Marty Staff. "It became very compartmentalized . . . more structured. The only one who knew everything that was going on was Gabriella, not even Calvin or Barry knew, in my opinion."

A source close to the company argued that this division was a good thing.

Before, "everybody reported to both Barry and Calvin, at least on the management level," the source said. "She put some great things in place—great structure in a sense that Calvin didn't have to be the decision maker on everything. I definitely know Barry appreciated her involvement, because he had a partner." She did this to free up Calvin's time so he could focus on design.

Soon after she started at Calvin Klein, the whole merchandise team had a meeting with the top brass at Saks Fifth Avenue to present the "new Calvin Klein."

The Saks contingent included Chairman Phil Miller, President Rose Marie Bravo, and Men's Fashion Director Stan Tucker, a former insider recalled.

"Let me understand, Gabriella," Bravo said, after the meeting had gone on for a while, "You made very clear your role, but what is Calvin's role going to be from now on?"

"Well," Forte answered, "I am the president of the company and Calvin is the head of the design studio. If you go to Calvin with any business issues, I'm going to be very pissed."

According to the insider, Klein said nothing.

Relations between the other strong woman in Calvin Klein's life, Linda Wachner, and Forte were rocky from the start.

After several months at Calvin Klein, Forte burst into Schwartz's office, where several execs were having an after-work chat over some wine.

"You tell that woman," she yelled, "you tell that woman I'm the fucking president of this company, and she better return my calls!" And with that she slammed the door on her way out.

Schwartz looked at John Kourakos, president of Warnaco's underwear division, and pleaded, "John, please go to Linda. Tell her that as a favor to Calvin and myself, to please, please return Gabriella's phone calls."

The next day, a former insider recounted, Kourakos returned from seeing Linda Wachner with a note for Schwartz that read, "I pay you two fucks $68 million [sic] for your company, and you expect me to talk to an underling?"

And that was just the start of their relationship.

"Between Gabriella, Calvin, and Linda Wachner, you had three of the most volcanic personalities in the industry," a former exec explained. "They each had their own perspectives on things.

"In some ways, I think Gabriella was outdone in management style by Linda Wachner. And Linda, because Calvin had sold his underwear license, had an upper hand in an area that Gabriella could do nothing about. Calvin swung a little bit like a pendulum" between the two respected women execs.

Forte's management style was an attraction for some and a repellent for others. The revved-up Calvin Klein, Inc., became a prime poacher on Seventh Avenue. Denise Seegal was one of the first to jump ship, from DKNY, to join Calvin Klein, Inc., to become president of its men's and women's cK division.

However, just as many jumped ship from Calvin Klein, Inc. The first to leave was advertising and creative services exec Neil Kraft. The second departure was a real blow to the company.

Susan Sokol, president of Calvin Klein collection, resigned in March 1995, saying it was "time to move on." Insiders, however, said the 23-year veteran, who was one of Schwartz and Klein's first employees, resigned under fire from Forte.

"Susan Sokol had an exalted role in the company, and it was justified," one former exec said. "Gabriella kept talking about Susan's age, not in an illegal way, but in a pointed way."

"Susan, you are the *grande* dame of the women's wear business in America right now," Gabriella chided, though she was very close in age to Sokol.

"Susan was a little vain and she liked to look young," the exec explained. "That's really attacking her in the worst place, and Gabriella would do it in every meeting."

To replace her, Forte hired Bloomingdale's vice president

Brenda Moser, which set off a firestorm. Bloomingdale's parent company Federated Department Stores had a long-standing policy against vendors hiring away its executives, which Forte and Moser disregarded. Consequently, the retail chain stopped carrying the high-end women's collection for several years.

Soon thereafter, jeans president Daniel Gladstone, underwear president John Kourakos, menswear president Marty Staff, and public relations vice president Lynn Tesoro all departed. It was a changing of the guard.

The deals that would potentially make Calvin Klein a player on the international scene were fast and furious in coming.

First was the creation of a partnership between Calvin Klein, Inc., and four Japanese companies in 1994. Though this venture, Calvin Klein Japan, was negotiated by Barry Schwartz at the same time the company was negotiating with Gabriella Forte to join the company, she nonetheless threw herself into it as soon as she arrived at Calvin Klein, getting it up and running to her specifications.

The partnership was created to establish licenses for all levels of the company's products. Expectations were lofty: Sales volume for the men's and women's collection, cK Calvin Klein sportswear, cK Calvin Klein jeans, and other licensed products were expected to reach $3 billion by 2006. CK Japan also expected to open 12 stores by 1999.

The company created a similar company, though without partners, for Europe the following year. Calvin Klein Europe was created to control distribution of licensed products and develop a strategy for selling collection and cK Calvin Klein sportswear.

Licenses were signed with Fratini SpA to manufacture and sell jeans in Europe and with Stefanel SpA to manufacture

In the early days, Calvin Klein would do just about anything for his customers, including travel to Scranton, Pennsylvania, for a benefit fashion show in 1970. From left, Calvin Klein, Mrs. Herman Goodman, owner of the Scranton Tribune Newspapers, and Vincent Rebicek. (*Photo credit:* Vincent Rebicek, ASID)

The kidnapping of Calvin Klein's daughter, Marci, was first suspected to be a publicity stunt to support the launch of his new designer jeans in 1978. Here, the designer is addressing the media from the FBI's offices.

Brooke Shields's billboard in Times Square stopped traffic and infuriated women's rights groups in 1980. (*Photo credit:* Walter McBride/Retna Ltd.)

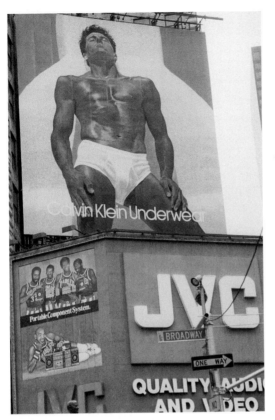

The billboard that changed the way the male body was treated in advertising. Tom Hintinaus, clad in very little Calvin Klein, high above Times Square in 1983. (*Photo credit:* Bettman/Corbis)

Calvin Klein was concerned with keeping himself in underwear-model shape. (*Photo credit:* Dan Brinzac/*New York Post*)

Calvin Klein's post-divorce jaunts to the gym paid off. (*Photo credit:* Abe Frajndlich/Retna Ltd.)

Klein, with Brooke Shields and Elizabeth Taylor at an AIDS benefit in 1985, achieved a level of celebrity many designers strive for. (*Photo credit:* Walter McBride/Retna Ltd.)

Calvin Klein with design assistant and girlfriend Kelly Rector, right. Staffers knew that Rector had spent the night at the designer's apartment when she wore the same outfit two days in a row. (*Photo credit:* John Barrett/*Globe*)

Klein and Rector married in an impromptu ceremony in Rome during a business trip in 1986. (*Photo credit:* AP/Wide World Photos)

Calvin Klein showed his all-American minimalism at Harvey Nichols in London. (*Photo credit:* Clive Dixon/Rex)

Vogue editor Anna Wintour, here with Calvin Klein, is possibly the most powerful person in the fashion business. (*Photo credit:* Rose Hartman/*Globe*)

Signature model Kate Moss injected a new level of reality into Calvin
Klein's advertising. (*Photo credit:* Patrick McMullan)

By capitalizing on rapper
Marky Mark's penchant for
dropping his trousers
onstage, Calvin Klein forged
the ultimate marriage
between pop music and fashion in 1993. (*Photo credit:*
Michael Cali/Rex)

As muses to Calvin Klein, Carolyn Bessette (later JFK Jr.'s wife) and wife Kelly Rector Klein filled different needs for the designer. (*Photo credit:* Patrick McMullan)

The designer and his wife Kelly, one year before their separation. (*Photo credit: Globe)*

The ads for Calvin Klein children's underwear lasted less than 24 hours in Times Square after the designer pulled them due to public outcry in 1999. (*Photo credit:* Elizabeth Lippman)

Though she complained bitterly about the kids' underwear ads, Warnaco's Linda Wachner, left, was all smiles several months later. (*Photo credit:* Sonia Moskowitz/*Globe*)

Calvin Klein, right, greeting customers at his new Madison Avenue store as his childhood friend and business partner Barry Schwartz looks on. (*Photo credit:* Rose Hartman/Globe)

The father of the bride escorts daughter Marci down the aisle for her marriage to model-turned-carpenter and part-time surfer Scott Murphy on Saturday, October 28, 2000. (*Photo credit:* Charles Sykes/Rex)

Calvin Klein's CFDA Lifetime Achievement Award in 1991 was marred by the tofu-cream pie that splattered the designer, his estranged wife Kelly, and friend, humorist Fran Lebowitz, left. (*Photo credit:* Sonia Moskowitz/*Globe*)

Calvin Klein, Inc., chairman Barry Schwartz split his time between Calvin and the New York Racing Association, where he served as chairman for the last two years he worked at the company. (*Photo credit:* Francis Specker/*New York Post*)

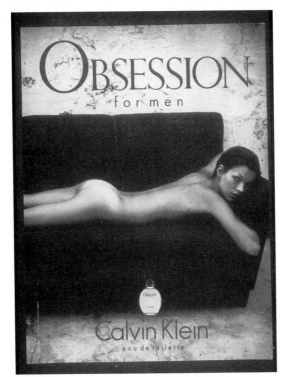

Breaking advertising
barriers for years,
Calvin Klein cleared
the way for designer
Tom Ford's provoca-
tive ads for Gucci.
(*Photo credit:* The
Advertising Archive,
Ltd.)

Calvin Klein has come
full circle. New signature
model Natalia Vodianova,
left, is the separated-at-
birth twin of the young
Brooke Shields, above.
(*Photo credit:* Shields,
Barbara Laing/*Globe;*
Vodianova, David
Rentas/*New York Post*)

He's still got it. Calvin Klein's celebrity still attracts women like Bianca Jagger, above, and starlet Gwyneth Paltrow, right. The designer provided Paltrow with clothes even before she was a box office draw. (*Photo credit:* Jagger, Fashion Wire Daily/Retna; Paltrow, Patrick McMullan)

Calvin Klein is known for his stellar A-list front row. Academy Award nominee Renée Zellweger, left, joined daughter Marci Klein and Academy Award winner Hillary Swank, right, at the designer's February 2003 show. (*Photo credit:* Andrea Renault/*Globe*)

The swans grace the runway for Calvin Klein's finale. (*Photo credit:* Fashion Wire Daily/Retna)

The wistful designer takes what most believe was his last stroll on the catwalk in February, 2003. (*Photo credit:* Elizabeth Lippman)

One month later, the designer has a very public meltdown at a New York Knicks basketball game. (*Photo credit:* Anthony Causi)

and sell cK Calvin Klein sportswear in Europe and the Middle East. The Stefanel agreement also included a license for opening a chain of cK stores throughout Europe, starting in 1997.

Korea was next on the Klein and Forte's list. The company signed an agreement with Shinsegae International Company to open freestanding collection and cK stores starting in fall 1996.

The designer wanted to have flagship stores in all of the European capitals. The designer chose a location for cK Calvin Klein on New Bond Street in London first, which was quickly followed by a collection store in Paris on Avenue Montaigne. Stores were eventually opened in Milan and Rome.

The pace at which these deals were done was dizzying. It seemed a lot could be accomplished when Forte ran the company 20 hours a day. However, what appeared to be the thorough execution of an ambitious strategic plan to the outside was seen as an impossible task to those on the inside. The infrastructure to support these initiatives didn't exist.

"The Stefanel business was a huge execution," recalled a source. "Gabriella orchestrated an amazing partnership, but it was too big for a true undertaking. The conceptual partnership was there, [but] the execution was bigger than the money [available] to make it happen. It launched and then it petered out.

"The licensees in Asia and the Pacific panhandle were developing a whole thing as well," but, the source added, "It just never really got to the point, or level, where it wanted to be."

When trend watcher Faith Popcorn professed that "cocooning" would be the wave of the future, Klein took it to heart.

Never one to miss a trend, Calvin Klein wanted to go home. The designer had dabbled in home furnishings over the years, with licenses for sheets, towels, and other accessories coming and going piecemeal, but by 1994, he was serious about it.

The company entered into an agreement with Home Innovations, Inc., to create a complete collection under the label "Calvin Klein Home." Scheduled to debut at retail in fall 1995, the collection would include everything from bed and bath, furniture, and dinnerware to wallpaper, glassware, and floor coverings.

"The vibrant core of modern life is home life," Klein said at the time, adding that the collection would reflect the same modern, minimalist designs as his clothing.

CHAPTER 11

Controversial cK

The success of cK Calvin Klein sportswear can be attributed to its simplicity. The clothing was pared-down vintage Calvin Klein—basic pieces that worked together or when combined with jeans. It wasn't revolutionary. It didn't set the world on its ear. It was just real—unfussy—which became an allure all its own.

The lack of pretense appealed perfectly to the generation of young adults coming of age in the early 1990s. Generation X, as it was called, was incredibly different from its predecessors in the 1970s "Me" generation or its greedy counterparts in the 1980s. Gen Xers wanted to be considered individuals. They were looking for a deeper meaning in life beyond designer labels, lofty titles, and hefty paychecks. They wanted something real, whether that was a socially conscious job, an environment-friendly car, or affordable clothes without ostentatious labels and logos.

As he has been known to do, Klein seized the moment and interpreted it in a new fragrance.

Klein had most recently launched Escape in 1991, which was the natural progression for the Klein brands. Obsession worked in the 1980s, Eternity conveyed a warm, fuzzy renewed morality, and Escape took you away from the pressures of the recession-plagued 1990s. It smelled like a vacation at the beach.

However, traditional fragrance-launch tactics were not going to appeal to the far-from-traditional Gen Xers. While Klein believed the company should create a fragrance for this group, shadows of doubt crept into his thought process. He shared his doubts one evening with a group of colleagues informally gathered in Barry Schwartz's office for an end-of-day glass of wine.

"Forget about the fragrance," Klein said. "People don't need another fragrance. People don't need more in their medicine cabinet.

"If there's a fragrance it should be simple," the designer continued. "It should not be expensive, and it should be the same for him and for her. It shouldn't even have a name or a theme or a message. It should just be cK one."

Marketing exec Pablo de Echevarria said silence came over the room with the realization that they had just watched the birth of the concept. "That was it," he said, "it was so insane."

The resulting fragrance, cK one, was a departure from tradition in every way. The scent itself was a fresh mix of spices, fruits, and musk. The top notes consisted of bergamot, cardamom, pineapple, and papaya. The middle notes were jasmine, violet, rose, and nutmeg. Two types of musk mixed with amber and green tea were pervasive throughout the scent. The fragrance technically was missing its bottom notes, which did two things—it made it cheaper to produce and it cut down on the scent's ability to last. Consequently, the fragrance needed to be reapplied every two hours, increasing usage, ultimately increasing sales.

Meant for both sexes, the clean, pure fragrance was not particularly masculine or feminine. Its packaging conveyed its "shared," not unisex, status. The bottle, a sandblasted glass flask with an aluminum top, resembled a small liquor bottle. The outside packaging was made of simple corrugated cardboard. It was unlike anything anyone had ever seen.

"The goal on cK one was to reinvent the way that fragrances were launched," said an executive who worked on the launch, "as they did when they launched Obsession—Obsession pushed image advertising. It was the biggest thing to happen to fragrance until cK one."

Calvin Klein Cosmetics looked at every step of the traditional launch formula and threw it out the window, particularly since cK one was targeting the younger consumer. "They had to go to where the younger consumer was, and they weren't really shopping in department stores," recalled the executive.

It was decided cK one would be sold where kids go and hang out—Tower Records—in a specially designed fixture that would allow customers to serve themselves, breaking another tenet of the fragrance industry. "No one had done open-sell in fragrances," the executive said.

The company worked to create a custom fixture for cK one, which the company adapted for cK clothing products like dress shirts and ties. Referred to as the "ISID fixture," de Echevarria once questioned the designers about its name.

"I know it's a technical term, but what does ISID mean?" he asked, after dealing with the jargon for weeks.

"You want this fixture to do so much, we call it 'It Slices It Dices,' " the fixture designer replied.

Regardless of its name, according to de Echevarria, "It was a huge success," for fragrance and men's shirts and ties.

Sales expectations for the scent were in the range of $20 million wholesale for the fall launch period. However, the shared fragrance smashed sales records, with receipts exceeding $5 million in its first 10 days, a company executive said.

With sales reaching levels more than double what was expected, the demand exceeded the amount of available product. A frenzy ensued, with people offering to buy bottles without the box or bottles that had been returned, "because everybody was out of stock," said the executive.

In the cosmetics and fragrance business, buying products that have been returned is unheard of. "Normally when things are returned, they go back to the supplier and they have a responsibility to destroy them," the executive said. The demand for cK one overrode business as usual.

"It was the thing (at the time), and it smelled good. Everybody was a cK one person. You couldn't walk down the street in 1994 and not smell it," recalled the executive.

The advertising also broke from tradition. Instead of romanticized or glamorous images, the campaign featured groups of people who looked real. Though the group included models Kate Moss and Jenny Shimizu, an Asian woman with a crew cut, it also featured members of the young Hollywood set, like Donovan Leitch and Michelle Hicks, that Gen Xers could identify with. The advertisements showed these groups chatting and interacting in serious or amusing conversations reminiscent of the Richard Avedon photo series, "Andy Warhol and Members of the Factory" done in 1969.

Calvin Klein blitzed America with the cK one images through print ads, outdoor ads, and television, all shot by

Steven Meisel in clean, stark black and white. And though the campaign as originally planned was enormous at $15 million, the unexpectedly high sales caused it to grow.

Because the license for fragrance dictated that a percentage of sales be applied to advertising and marketing, "we ended up with all this money that needed to be spent by the end of the year so that the books would even out," the executive said.

Consequently, "we got to do a lot of really cool advertising and promotions, like the Metrocard," the executive recalled, citing an ad buy through New York's Transit Authority. Still, people couldn't get enough of the imagery. "People were breaking bus shelters in Manhattan to steal the posters out of them."

While cK one was dominating the fragrance world with its stunning sales and stark black-and-white images, Calvin Klein was devising a new advertising campaign to show off its cK jeans and underwear.

The 116-page rock 'n' roll supplement the company created to put Calvin Klein Jeans back on the map four years before did little to spur sales after an initial spark. The problem, Klein believed, was that cK jeans weren't important to teenagers—the only consumers buying his jeans were parents of the teenagers and longtime customers. The company needed a campaign that would set that straight.

"What everybody agreed on is that it needed to be geared to the 15-year-old," recalled marketing exec de Echevarria. "After much research, much comparison, and debating strategies," the designer had a revelation.

"If you want kids to like you, you need to piss off their parents," Klein said.

"The original idea was Calvin's—just to piss the parents off," de Echevarria echoed. "But guess what? The response was just ridiculous. The jeans [sales] exploded."

The designer was not alone in his decision to run the ads—his trusted adviser, wife Kelly, believed in them.

"Those were the ads Kelly wanted done but nobody else did," said an ex-employee. "The reason Calvin went ahead with them, even though the ad agency and everybody told him not to do it . . . is that Kelly is not just his muse, but his biggest influence . . . whatever she says he'll do."

"She's been known to influence him in not so many good ways," said another former employee. "He did respect her judgment."

Famed fashion photographer Steven Meisel, riding high on his success with Madonna's *Sex* book and the recent cK one campaign, was asked to shoot Klein's new campaign. Sticking with the "real people" theme that worked so well for cK one, the ads featured kids, or actors who looked like kids, in an intentionally cheesy setting.

Posed in a 1970s setting of wood paneling and shabby shag carpeting, the print campaign showed the kids posed in provocative positions. One girl was shown lying on the floor with her skirt hiked up to reveal her stark white panties; another was shown touching her breasts while wearing jeans and a denim vest. A boy posed with his legs splayed so that his underwear showed from beneath his denim shorts.

While these were provocative, the corresponding television campaign was much worse. It brought the seedy environment to life with astounding clarity. Instead of the actors communicating with each other, there was a lascivious off-camera voice asking questions and giving direction. The off-camera voice originally belonged to none other than Lou Maletta, a fixture on the New York public access cable circuit known for his shows *In the Dungeon,* about sado-masochistic fetishists, and *Men & Films,* clips from hard-core gay films. Though a concerned Klein replaced Maletta with a voice-over actor at the eleventh hour, the tone remained the same.

The interaction portrayed was understood to be a casting for a pornographic movie.

"Are you strong?" a man's offscreen voice asked a young James Dean look-alike.

"I like to think so," the boy eagerly answered.

"Do you think you could rip that shirt off of you?" The boy then grabbed his shirt at the neck and tore the T-shirt in half, revealing a skinny, pubescent chest.

"That's a nice body. Do you work out?"

"Mmm hmm."

A lascivious cackle comes from offscreen, "Yeah, I can tell."

The print ads, placed in the August issue of teen magazine *YM,* initially set off media watchers, particularly when Janice Grossman, publisher of *Seventeen,* said her magazine wouldn't have accepted the ad if they'd been approached (they weren't).

A spokesman for Calvin Klein defended the company's strategy: "Young people are trend setters. We think the campaign approaches jeans in a way that they wear them."

Each new facet of the campaign, first the television ads and then the outdoor and bus ads, was greeted with outcries dutifully reported by the media. Reports that the television ads were being banned from the airwaves spurred the designer to issue a statement on August 10, 1995, four days before the ads were scheduled to hit the airwaves, explaining the company's position.

"Some people have been surprised by the look of the ads because they don't have a slick, glamorous setting," Klein

said in a written statement. "The whole point of this campaign is that people, regular people from anywhere, like the
kid we have from Kentucky or the girl from Germany, have
glamour inside of them—which is tied to their independence. And you can find it anywhere, not just at a modeling
agency or movie studio.

"We are stunned that anyone could find these ads pornographic. If someone finds that these ads are pornographic,
then they are reading something into them that was never
intended," the company said in a subsequent statement.

"The inspiration of the new jeans campaign was the idea
of amateurism and media awareness—and the strength of
personality and self-knowledge of young people today."

Regardless of the reaction, the campaign's blitz on the
city became more prevalent with each successive day. The
ads appeared on 250 New York City buses starting on August 15, which took the complaints to the next level and
brought a protest to Calvin Klein's headquarters.

Noach Dear, a former New York City councilman repre-
senting Brooklyn, mobilized the first protest against the ads
in the form of a press conference a week later, which was
held outside Calvin Klein, Inc., headquarters at 205 West
39th Street, off the southern side of Times Square.

"All kinds of people joined us," he recalled, including
some "big goons" from Calvin Klein, "to try to scare us."

However, Dear and his group didn't get the response
they were looking for. In fact, they didn't get any response
from Calvin Klein.

"After the press conference, we decided no one [at the
company] was listening. So we said, 'Let's try a boycott.' "
However, he added, there was risk involved with the threat.
"Boycotts are very touchy things—you can fall flat on your
face," but, "the last thing you want is anyone saying anything bad about your product."

The proposed boycott coupled with calls from the American Family Association to reveal the ages of the models used in the campaign spurred the company into action.

Calvin Klein ran a full-page advertisement in the *New York Times* explaining its decision to abandon the campaign and issued the following statement: "We made the decision after going through a constructive dialog with different people regarding the ads. We explained to them that we wanted to get across a message about the independence and strength of character of young people today and about the inner glamour that regular people everywhere can have. We listened and talked to them about the concerns that they raised and in the process, it became evident that the ads weren't conveying the message we hoped. Because our customers are of paramount importance to us, we took their concerns seriously and acted on them."

While the ads were withdrawn from television, buses, and magazines, the firestorm had just begun.

The Calvin Klein offices were still under siege from the media, with crews and reporters camped out in front of the office. For employees, that meant they were held captive in the offices from the time they entered until the end of the day. "We were told not to say anything under penalty of being fired," an ex-employee said. "You had to say 'no comment' and that's it."

However, "no comment" was the last thing the company wanted to say about its new flagship store, scheduled to open September 7 in the midst of the "kiddie porn" brouhaha.

Opening a New York flagship store was a longtime aspiration for Calvin Klein. Since the late 1980s he'd been looking for the perfect location to show all of his products under one roof.

Finally, in early summer 1994, Klein signed a deal for a space on Madison Avenue and 60th Street, on the same block as Barneys New York. The three-level store, a former bank, offered 20,000 square feet of selling space Klein intended to fill with the men's and women's collection, shoes, accessories, sportswear, underwear, fragrance, and the company's new home furnishings. In short, it would give the designer a showcase for all his wares, and as such, it had to be perfectly designed to Klein's specifications, which in one case specifically was a challenge.

To fit the Calvin Klein brand image, the designer wanted a particular concrete floor.

"The floor needs to be raw cement, without any kind of sealer," Klein said.

The contractors disagreed with the designer. The floor needed a sealer or it would disintegrate and become dusty with regular use.

"I don't care," Klein said. "That's the look that I want!" Hundreds of alternative cement samples were offered to Klein for his inspection, but none of them were up to snuff. Finally, he said, "If a store downtown can do it, why can't we do it?"

The downtown store Klein mentioned was contacted about its floor and, not surprisingly, "there was a sealer," a former insider said. "We put on a sealer without him knowing." The insider added, "Klein's great, because he knows what he wants and he goes for it, but constantly testing your loyalty, testing how far he can push it."

Challenges like finding the right concrete pushed the store's planned opening from March 1995 to September 7, 1995. Not only did this cause the company to lose sales every day it didn't open, it landed the opening smack dab in the middle of the company's kiddie porn controversy.

For the designer who had become known for his legendary control—of the brand, of his licenses, and of his
image—this coincidence was a disaster in the making.
Though he and his staff made every effort to control the
press and its access, inquiries about the controversy slipped
through.

Don Kaplan, a former reporter for the *Daily News Record,*
the brother to *WWD,* was sent to interview the designer during the hullabaloo.

"I got the assignment to go over there and talk about the
store," Kaplan recalled. In arranging for the interview, the
publicist stated that questions about the advertising scandal
were off limits. "Of course, I was going to leave this for my
last question, so I could get my story done and then, if I
could, get more out of him," Kaplan said.

Kaplan admitted being immediately intimidated by Klein's
office. "It was really strange . . . everything's white," including the round table the designer used for a desk and the klieg
light behind him. The interview was being monitored by a
"very tall beautiful PR woman" whom Kaplan believed was
Carolyn Bessette.

The interview progressed as expected until Kaplan's last
question.

"I finally said to him, do you think that all this negative
publicity associated with your ad campaign is going to have
any effect on the store's sales in the first couple of weeks?"
Kaplan recalled. "There was complete silence, even the
blond stopped writing and looked at him, he looked at her."

Klein smacked the table with his hands. "The interview is
over," he said.

And then the publicist "grabs me by the shoulder and
escorts me out of the office," Kaplan said. The reporter was
scheduled to get a walk-though of the new store later that

afternoon, and though the Klein camp called Kaplan's editor to complain even before he'd returned to the office, the later appointment was still on.

When he met the designer at the store, "it was as if nothing had happened," Kaplan said. It was "perfectly nice and all smooth." Even when Klein tripped and fell hard against a glass wall, the designer "kept walking like nothing had happened," Kaplan said, adding, "it was like watching a performer; I've never seen anything like it."

Though the advertisements had been pulled, the question that fueled the fervor was whether the kids in the ads were old enough to have consented to making them. The American Family Association was fueling the fire by asking Attorney General Janet Reno to launch an investigation based on the exploitation of the children by "exhibiting them in a lascivious manner," although the models were not completely nude.

The Justice Department admitted that it convened a preliminary investigation to explore the specifics of the campaign, not on the urging of the American Family Association, but after FBI employees started seeing the ads on city buses in New York.

The Klein camp continued to profess its innocence. "We're very confident that we've violated no laws," a spokesman said. "It is sheer demagoguery to suggest otherwise."

While the Justice Department was conducting its investigation, then president Bill Clinton even weighed in. "I don't have any comment on whether those Calvin Klein ads were legal or illegal," the president told attendees to a fund-raising dinner in Denver. "Those children were my daughter's age that were [sic] in those ads, and they were outrageous. It was wrong. It was wrong to manipulate those children and use them for commercial benefit."

Still, through all of this, Klein still didn't understand why there was such an uproar. "We did a fragrance ad with frontal nudity, and that is acceptable in some magazines," he said, referring to past campaigns. "These people have more clothes on. . . . People didn't get that it's about modern young people who have an independent spirit and do the things they want to and can't be told or sold. None of that came though."

By early November 1995, the Justice Department decided that no federal laws were violated by the ads, clearing Klein of any suspicion, which unceremoniously ended the witch hunt.

The real question is whether this campaign actually did what it was supposed to—drive younger consumers to buy cK jeans. While the company did not release sales figures, anecdotal evidence suggested it did push teens into the stores.

Calvin Klein, Inc., however, had moved onto its next in-your-face advertising campaign. An advertisement for under-wear featured 20-year-old model Joel West, in white briefs, sitting on the floor with his legs wide apart. While it didn't draw criticism from morals groups, it drew ire from War-naco's Linda Wachner, who manufactured the underwear and paid for the ad.

"This ad," she bristled to *WWD*, "was not approved by Warnaco. When I saw the original artwork, I said no!"

Wachner actually consulted her attorneys over the matter, but both she and Calvin Klein went out of their way to con-firm they were staying in business together. Still, it was the start of trouble Klein and Schwartz would deal with for years to come.

A source close to the company felt the Joel West ad was created specifically to push buttons in the aftermath of cK jeans. "To me that was in your face . . . unnecessary," Wachner said. "That to me wasn't a vision. That was to be controversial."

To follow up on the unprecedented success of cK one, Calvin Klein Cosmetics created a new fragrance, cK be, which launched in the late summer of 1996. Once again, this was to be a "shared" fragrance, described as a "fresh tonic musk," with top notes of bergamot, juniper berry, mandarin, mint, and lavender, with magnolia and peach at the heart, and sandalwood, opoponax, and tonka bean at its base.

Expectations for this fragrance were set higher based on the off-the-charts success of cK one. Sales were expected to be in the $30 million range for its first season, with an estimated $20 million devoted to advertising.

Instead of the groups of people hanging out that represented cK one, cK be is about one person, just being. It is "a close up look at the individuals within the cK group," the company said.

The supporting advertising campaign was larger than anything the company had done before. Television, print, and outdoor advertising was bought in addition to new media, like hydro-illuminations, which projected images onto a thin wall of mist, and also 8 million ticket backs for Ticketmaster events in September and October 1996.

The problem with the all-pervasive cK be campaign is that it appeared to glorify drug use and anorexia. The models featured in the campaign were skinny to the point of being unhealthy-looking. Their hair was stringy and unstyled; their tattoos, scars, piercings, and blemishes uncovered for all to see. One "model" even appeared to have track marks. "I've squatted. I've begged. I'm the real thing," bragged one model, Billy White.

The campaign, being all about individuality, got the point across, particularly through the script for the television commercials.

"Be a saint. Be a sinner. Just be," said one tattooed love god.

A longer version digs deeper. "You could get hurt. You could get sick. You could do all these things, and if you don't have intimate relationships that are strong, you're really alone. But alone is something I know how to do. Intimacy comes and goes. Alone is forever. Be single. Be plural. Just be," recites a not unhappy young man.

This campaign hit the airwaves and pages when young culture was at a crossroads. The discontent of Generation X had taken on enormous proportions. They watched themselves, or close facsimiles, wade through angst on MTV's *Real World* and *Road Rules,* and they seemed to want out. Raves graduated from the underground to the mainstream, and the drug of choice, ecstasy, made everything better. It was hard not to love everyone while you were high on the hallucinogenic drug. Many used this discontent as an excuse for trying harder drugs, and heroin chic was born.

Klein tapped into this cultural need for differentiation with his cK be campaign. It showed these people as they were. The problem was that the kids who weren't like the models in the campaign strived to be so. Klein was charged with glorifying anorexia and drug use, and worse, by the media.

Former president Bill Clinton weighed in again on Klein's creative. "The glorification of narcotics is not creative, it's destructive," he said at the time. "We have come to see children as a class of people as something to be marketed. Maybe I'm just getting old fashioned, but I just came out of my shoes when I saw those teenagers depicted the way they were in those Calvin Klein ads. I thought it was wrong."

While many people agreed with the then president, many consumers bought into the whole notion of cK be, pumping up its sales to match those of cK one when it launched.

Calvin Klein seemed to be taking an uncharacteristic step back from the launch of cK be. Normally very supportive of fragrance launches, the designer seemed to be spending more time on his personal life, taking time at his house in East Hampton with his wife of nine years, Kelly. However, the reality couldn't have been any further from the truth.

In August 1996, the couple announced they were separating.

"We are still the best of friends," they said in a joint statement. "We have made a decision to live apart. We are respectful of one another. We hope to work out any issues between ourselves."

And while rumors and innuendo about his sexuality constantly plagued the designer throughout his career, people who saw the couple together believed there was real affection between them—that it wasn't an arrangement.

"They were very loving and natural," a former employee recalled. "He relaxed with her. Physically, you could see him breathe a sigh of relief when she was there."

Klein apparently was going through a painful time and just wanted to be left alone, whether in the office or in his flagship store. In fact, in both places, staff was told not to address him, say hello, or look him in the eye, under threat of being fired.

CHAPTER 12

The Trouble with Linda

Though the big cK jeans advertising campaign turned out to be a public relations fiasco, the sale of Calvin Klein Sport, including the jeans business, to Arnold Simon's Rio Sportswear and Charter House Equity Partners was nothing less than a rousing success.

Simon, a burly man who kept a 300-gallon fish tank filled with poisonous varieties in his office, renamed the partnership Designer Holdings, Ltd. in February 1996. He instituted some logical changes that made all the difference in allowing the business to grow considerably. He lowered the price of the jeans, increased the number of basic styles offered, and changed the fit to broaden its target audience. On the retail side, Designer Holdings developed rapid-response programs so that retailers never ran low on stock. The subsequent results were stunning. Annual sales in 1995 were $361.4 million versus the $59 million rung up in 1993, the last year Calvin Klein, Inc., controlled the jeans business.

In the mid-1990s, the stock markets in the United States

experienced incredible growth fueled by the Internet and Web-based businesses. The potential payoff lured all kinds of investors into the market, from professional to plebe. Companies, seeing the potential, all strived for one thing— going public. By making an initial public offering, a company could generate mountains of cash to pay down debt, fund expansion, or simply line executives' pockets. Companies like Charter House Equity Partners invested in deals and formed partnerships knowing that there could be an IPO payday down the road if properly managed.

It came as no surprise when Designer Holdings made the filings required for an initial public offering in March 1996. The company hoped to generate about $68.4 million for its owners, Charter House and Simon, which controlled 96 percent of the company, and its six smaller investors.

It did come as a surprise to Calvin Klein, who, sources said, was unaware of Simon's plan. No doubt the designer was fuming, once again, that another was making money off his name and he was getting no part of it.

Designer Holdings could hardly have chosen a better time to go public. The market had IPO fever. Every company with a halfway decent product and an iota of growth potential was gearing up to make its debut. Fashion and retail companies, in particular, were looked at as sure things that would appeal to the common investor. The Gucci Group and Italian jeweler Bulgari were the first enter the fray in 1995, to much success. After all, if consumers had the choice to buy 100 shares in the XYZ Widget Company or 100 shares in the company that made their favorite jeans, shoes, or watch, most would choose the latter.

"The market is buying names and it's buying them big. The stocks are being snapped up on the basis of cachet and the reputation of the products," said *WWD*'s financial editor at the time, Sidney Rutberg. "It's glitz and prayers and hope. It's not really based on substance," he added.

Still, companies like Donna Karan, Saks Fifth Avenue, Abercrombie & Fitch, and Polo Ralph Lauren were all successfully following the IPO pattern.

The enthusiastic anticipation of Designer Holdings Ltd.'s debut on the New York Stock Exchange caused the company to up its initial offer from 10 million to 12 million shares. The price per share, originally expected to be in the $14 to $15 range, came in at $18, at the high end of the revised estimates. On its first day of trading, the issue was the second most actively traded stock, rising $7.75 to close at $25.75. Instead of raising $68 million for its backers, it generated a whopping $216 million. While it was a hard nut for Klein to swallow, he did get something.

Just prior to going public, Simon, Klein, and Schwartz went back to the bargaining table. The deal sewed up Designer Holdings possession of the Calvin Klein jeans license through 2040. In exchange, Klein and Schwartz got guaranteed increases on their royalty payments that would reach $22 million for the years 2031 through 2040. The duo from the Bronx also was given 1.28 million shares in the company, or 4 percent of total outstanding shares. The license deal was amended at that time to require less strict net-worth and debt-to-net-worth levels.

With the confidence of market investors behind him, Arnold Simon acquired a cocky swagger, businesswise, targeting those who were eating into his potential gains.

Counterfeiters, for instance, were the first he went after, through warehouse giant PriceCostco, Inc. Designer Holdings filed suit against the retailer charging that it was intentionally selling counterfeit merchandise and was also passing second-quality merchandise off as first-quality. The company filed a similar suit against Conway stores in New York.

As dictated by Klein and Schwartz, Calvin Klein had a strict policy of not selling to warehouse retailers to keep the brand's distribution channels clean and the name valuable. The objective of the lawsuits was not only to stop the selling of counterfeit merchandise, but also to get to and stop the counterfeiters. One year later, Designer Holdings hit the mother lode, with two separate seizures of counterfeit goods. Nine traffickers were arrested and more than 14,000 fake Calvin Klein garments were confiscated in raids in Hawthorne, California, and East Rutherford, New Jersey.

While the news of the raid was good, Simon had bigger fish to fry, as Designer Holdings had taken a wrong turn and Linda Wachner was calling.

After the company's stunning debut on the stock market, shares of Designer Holdings rose to a high of $34 before settling back down in the range of its IPO price of $18 by the end of the summer. There they stayed until spring 1997, when the company hit a number of snafus.

First, Simon had been in discussions with Donna Karan to manufacture its DKNY jeanswear through the fall of 1996. The deal was on, then the deal was off. The negotiations continued, then talks broke down completely, causing the stock of Designer Holdings to take a hit.

Second, a strategy to streamline the distribution of Calvin Klein jeans was seen as a negative by investors. In a move that was similar to a strategy Klein and Schwartz had used when the company was in its infancy, Simon proposed focusing the business on department stores and higher-end specialty stores to increase long-term profitability. However, he warned, sales and profits for fiscal 1996 would be affected by this move and the numbers would be flat. Wall Street didn't buy it.

In the age of quarterly fiscal accountability, the lack of improvement was not acceptable, and the stock took another hit, closing at $10.62 the day the news was released, and it kept dropping. It hit a low of $6.62 later that week.

While the company employed a number of tactics to raise the share price, including a stock buyback plan, it didn't move until talk of an acquisition hit the street.

Linda Wachner wanted another piece of the Calvin Klein business, and the time was right for her to go after it.

"We know how to create core basics," Wachner said at the time, referring to the jeans business. "We like to repeat what we know."

She had negotiated with Simon in 1995, but the two couldn't settle on a price because Simon's business was growing so fast. This time she had the upper hand.

Wachner's offer of $11 per share in Warnaco stock was accepted by Simon and his board, putting the value of the deal at $354 million. Upon completion, Wachner and Warnaco would be responsible for about one-third of the manufacturing and distribution of Klein's estimated $2.5 billion empire.

Warnaco's Calvin Klein underwear sales of $340 million in 1997 combined with annual sales of $470 million for Calvin Klein jeanswear added up to a lot of power for Wachner. It meant that the executive, already difficult to deal with, would hold sway over department stores and vendors, not to mention the designer himself.

Klein and Schwartz were concerned about having too much riding in one basket with Warnaco and were working behind the scenes to rustle up another bidder. However, none materialized, and with Klein not having any power to stop the sale, it was consummated.

While there was talk behind the scenes that Klein and Schwartz were dismayed at Wachner getting the jeans business, the problem was rooted more in their lack of ability to control the situation. However, since it wasn't the license, but rather the company that held the license, that was being sold, the deal was still in effect.

Certainly, the duo had concerns about working with a company that had no experience producing jeans. They were reassured that Simon was staying on to run the business, but days before Warnaco took possession, Wachner fired him, paying him $4.5 million in severance for six weeks' work. Still, when the time came, Klein saved face and joined in on an investor's conference call with Wachner and Simon.

"Obviously, Linda and Warnaco have been important in our underwear business," the designer said citing its great growth. "We are looking forward to continuing that in the jeans world."

The acquisition brought about a shift in the balance of power at Calvin Klein, where the tail was wagging the dog. Wachner was a demanding manager known for her long hours and merciless meeting schedule. There were regular calls from airplanes to reporters, meetings over manicures, visits to the Calvin Klein offices with her dog EBITDA (named after the accounting term), which inevitably resulted in messes for the assistants to clean up, and even calls from her bathtub in the evening.

"I remember meeting her for the first time," recalled a former insider. "I had to eat a frankfurter with sauerkraut at seven o'clock in the morning. That's the last thing I wanted to do," but the insider didn't have a choice. "She had so much control in a lot of ways."

Still, Klein and Schwartz kowtowed to Wachner, socializing

with her and even making her wardrobe season after season.

The problem was that Wachner was a slave to the bottom line. Even more than Klein and Schwartz, she wanted to make money—really big money—because she had shareholders clamoring for big growth every year. A strategy that involved reducing doors (i.e., the number of stores) to increase profits and prestige wouldn't fly at a company like Warnaco. Do what's best for Warnaco was the mantra, not what's best for the Calvin Klein brand. That could, and eventually did, mean trouble for the designer company.

It was feared in creative circles that Linda Wachner's growing importance at Calvin Klein, Inc., would put a damper on the edgy advertising the designer was known for. In the past, she had been vocal about not liking certain ads, the men's underwear advertisement featuring a legs-splayed Joel West, in particular. And though the licensing agreements specified creative control over design and marketing was the responsibility of Klein, Wachner was footing the bills. It was unlikely that an executive as opinionated as she was would not want to participate in the process.

The relationship was put to the test with the launch of Calvin Klein underwear for kids in February 1999. The company had planned a number of events around the launch, including an unveiling of its new Times Square billboard to take place on February 18, during New York's fashion week, and an in-store appearance with model Christy Turlington and the four children featured in the advertisements at Macy's Herald Square.

The day before the billboard was to be unveiled, local newspapers ran with stories that Calvin Klein was at it again, featuring children in his sexually provocative advertisements. And it was worse than the prior cK advertisements, because not only were they underwear-clad, but this time there was no disputing the fact that these were children, most under the age of six.

At a quick glance, the advertisements featured kids in a scene that probably happens every day in America. One ad featured two little girls in panties and undershirts jumping on a sofa, hand in hand. Another showed two boys, one wearing boxers, the other briefs, roughhousing on the sofa.

"I know with the creative, they did make a decision that it should only be single-sex . . . that it wouldn't be a boy and a girl jumping around, because then that would be sort of lascivious," a company source recalled. "They felt it was safe having kids playing like they do at home, jumping around in underwear, while the mother is trying chase them around and get them dressed. It was meant to be a wholesome ad—it wasn't meant to be anything scandalous."

The problems with the ads were numerous, as were the complaints—the ads sexualized children, they were provocative in a shameful way, the boy wearing briefs was shot to look as though he had an erection, and so on. The problem most cited, though, was the picture of the two boys roughhousing. If you glanced at the boy wearing boxers quickly, it appeared as though his genitals were exposed. On closer inspection, you could determine that what you actually saw was his hand. However, the damage was done.

"In professional advertising, nothing is allowed without a purpose," said Bob Peters, president of Morality in Media, a watchdog organization. "You really had to look twice to see it wasn't his penis. In my opinion, it was purposeful. You didn't have to be an Albert Einstein to figure out that they hadn't overlooked the fact that the little boy's finger was positioned in such a way as to look like his penis."

Rosie O'Donnell blasted the ad during the live taping of her top-rated television program the same day. Showing the advertisement in the March 1999 issue of *Martha Stewart Living* on her show, the comedienne told her audience, "I'll never wear his underwear again."

That was the deciding factor for the Klein camp. At the time, O'Donnell could do no wrong in the eyes of Middle America. Her show's ratings were unprecedented, and she herself was seen as the poster child for the wholesome middle classes. An advocate for anything having to do with children, hers was a powerful opinion that potentially carried massive weight at retail.

"The decision [to pull the campaign] came because of Rosie O'Donnell," the inside source said. "At that time, she had such power over people's opinions, especially in Middle America. If she was finding this objectionable," the company was in trouble.

After a day of fielding calls and making logistical contingency plans, the company announced that it was pulling the campaign. The company's announcement actually crossed the newswires at 10:17 P.M. on February 17, in time to make the evening news and late editions of the local newspapers in New York.

"The advertising campaign that we created to launch Calvin Klein Underwear for Kids was intended to show children smiling, laughing and just being themselves. We wanted to capture the same warmth and spontaneity that you find in a family snap-shot," the company said in its statement.

"The comments and reaction that we have received today raised issues that we had not fully considered. We are concerned by this response and appreciate the time that people have taken to contact us with their thoughts and opinions. As a result, we have decided to discontinue the campaign immediately." And with that, the billboard in Times Square came down as fast as it went up, with Klein appearing to have saved face.

Morality in Media's Peters, however, believes the company expected the results it got and planned for it.

"You know the old saying, 'Bad publicity is better than no publicity?' These companies do things knowing they're going to get beat up in the press," he explained. "They also know that in the process of getting beat up, they attract attention to their product."

Calvin Klein's strategy was interesting, Peters said, because of the company's cross-generational appeal.

"The primary audience is kids and young adults who think they're cool and want to be edgy. But at the same time, I'm sure a lot of adults buy [Calvin Klein] products." Through controversial ads, "they get the notoriety they want" with the kids and "they pull the ads to make themselves look half responsible" to adult customers. "And they got a billion dollars of free publicity," he added.

The designer eventually came around to see what the commotion was about, but it took a couple days.

"You see other people's ads with children in underwear," Klein said. "The reality is that if the name Calvin Klein is associated with it, it brings something else to the issue. He added, "I see that now."

Warnaco's Wachner, however, was more concerned with how the company would generate sales for the new collection. The only damage she was concerned with was to her bottom line, which became a problem for the Calvin Klein brand.

Warnaco owned the underwear business outright, which gave the company more leeway with its distribution than it had with Calvin Klein jeans, which it manufactured under a license that stipulated the types of retailers it could sell. Warnaco's Wachner took full advantage of this fact when she agreed to sell Calvin Klein underwear to JC Penney.

Officially considered a department store chain, JC Penney was at the low end of the spectrum, carrying little prestige with consumers. In the early 1990s, the company successfully embarked on a strategy to add brands to its mix of private label merchandise, but still catered to customers who were not buying high-end and designer brands.

The move to sell Calvin Klein underwear to JC Penney, while perhaps the right move to grow Warnaco's business, was perceived as a slap in the face to retailers like Macy's and Bloomingdale's. It cheapened the image of the Calvin Klein brand and was said to have infuriated Klein and Schwartz. However, they were powerless to do a thing.

One retailer even suggested it would take Calvin Klein down the road that destroyed designer Halston, who had signed a deal with JC Penney in the 1970s to design a lower-priced collection, Halston III, which would be exclusive to the retailer. At the time, JC Penney had no cachet whatsoever, and stores like Bergdorf Goodman dropped Halston's signature collection. The brand is still recovering from this gaffe.

CHAPTER 13

On the Block

With Gabriella Forte on board and friend and unofficial adviser David Geffen making suggestions from afar, Calvin Klein's long and painful repositioning from a manufacturing company to a design, marketing, and licensing company was a complete success. By the late 1990s, the company had hit its stride, with worldwide sales increasing with each successive year. From sales of $2.1 billion in 1994, to sales of $3.3 billion in 1995, to sales of $4.4 billion in 1996, the company peaked in 1997, with sales of more than $5 billion, before heading in the other direction.

This growth was the kind investors were desperate to see. The fashion IPO market was still hot even after the disappointing Donna Karan offering lost half its value after its debut, and industry watchers figured it was just a matter of time before Klein and Schwartz took the plunge.

The duo from the Bronx, however, had plans that didn't include going public. They had had enough of playing slave to quarterly statements when they had outstanding bonds in the 1980s. They wanted a bigger payday with fewer strings; they just had to figure out when the time was right.

The driver for much of this growth, Gabriella Forte, had reached the end of the line at Calvin Klein, Inc., by mid-1999. Her five-year contract had run out and was not renewed by Klein and Schwartz, though all professed to an amicable parting. Forte's reason for leaving was to spend more time with her family. However, she still had some deals—licenses—pending that allowed her to become a "strategic adviser" to the company.

"I'm not leaving the company," Forte told *WWD*. "I have willingly and gratefully stepped back from day-to-day operations, but I will still be involved in long-term plans and in all the projects I have developed at Calvin Klein."

The industry was aswirl with rumors about where the "terrible terrier" was going. The most circulated report had her going to work for Italian company Holding di Partecipazioni Industriali (HdP), owners of GFT, the licensee for Klein's men's suits. However, this position never materialized. Instead, her office was moved from the top executive floor to a "crappy office on a crappy floor," a source within said. "They took away what power she had."

Forte ended up where so many did at that time—working for an Internet company. Her particular concern was the now-defunct Beauty.com, while her position at Calvin Klein was filled by former Tahari exec, the even-tempered Tom Murry, who had been at Calvin Klein for three years as president of cK Calvin Klein.

The Internet and the businesses it spawned were pumping fortunes into the economy in 1999. The stock markets were the primary recipients of this wealth, but it filtered throughout other sectors, puffing up market capitalizations and personal investor portfolios across the world.

This era saw the birth of the fashion conglomerate. Bernard Arnault's LVMH Moet Hennessy Louis Vuitton was the first. Arnault took the spoils generated by liquor sales and pumped millions into faded luxury fashion brands like Christian Dior and Givenchy, revitalizing them in the process. Domenico De Sole followed suit with Gucci, and Prada's Patrizio Bertelli eventually entered the game as well.

Companies like these seemed to be playing a game of beat the clock with each other, coming up with almost a deal a day for the media, market watchers, and investors to sink their teeth into. As a result, mergers and acquisitions became the name of the game in the fashion industry, with everyone wanting a piece of the multi-billion-dollar pie. Venture capital was easy to come by, particularly when everyone saw a big IPO payday at the end of the road. These were manic times.

The duo from Mosholu Parkway, Calvin Klein and Barry Schwartz, saw the coincidence of peak market conditions with the company's superior fiscal condition as a sign the time was right to sell Calvin Klein, Inc.

In October 1999, Klein and Schwartz hired Lazard Freres & Co. as a financial consultant to, in so many words, put the company on the block.

Calvin Klein, Inc., was "undertaking a review of strategic courses of action," the company said in a release. "Strategic alternatives to be considered include a merger or similar business combination and strategic alliances."

According to Klein and Schwartz, "Our company is in a position of unprecedented competitive strength. We have made tremendous progress in recent years building our brand, products and infrastructure on a global basis . . . now is the ideal time to consider strategic alternatives that would enable us to capitalize fully in the many avenues of growth available to us."

The announcement unleashed an unprecedented amount of speculation on Wall Street and Seventh Avenue regarding who would buy the company and what the price would be.

The usual suspects were mentioned (LVMH, Gucci, Prada) and also some not-so-usual contenders—Liz Claiborne, Tommy Hilfiger, and Warnaco's Linda Wachner. For what amount, no one could guess, as conventional multiples of 15 to 10 times the company's income had faded away with the times. The competition to complete deals on Seventh Avenue was rendering heretofore standard formulas obsolete. LVMH's Bernard Arnault had previously offered $8 billion for Gucci, which was more than eight times its annual sales. Following that precedent, Klein and Schwartz could be offered $20 billion based on its expected $2.5 billion in sales for 1999.

Warnaco was touted as the first company in line. Buying the designer's company would save chief exec Wachner millions and millions of dollars in the long run, as she would not have to pay the designer large royalties if the brand were hers.

The next contenders were the Europeans. Bernard Arnault's LVMH had been on a fashion company buying spree. Fueled with $1.62 billion cash raised by selling a stake in the Diageo beverage company, LVMH was willing to spend money in 1999, acquiring both watch company Tag Heuer and Fendi through a joint venture with Prada.

Domenico De Sole's Gucci Group was next in line. De Sole and designer Tom Ford had masterminded the return of this illustrious Italian label to the top of the fashion heap. French retail concern Pinault Printemps Redoute (PPR) infused about

$3 billion into Gucci's coffers when it bought 42 percent of its shares. Gucci earmarked that war chest for acquisition and expansion, putting the company firmly in the running to buy Calvin Klein.

As an aside, Tom Ford may have had an emotional interest in acquiring Calvin Klein. More than 15 years younger than Klein, Ford was a fan of the designer when he was growing up and was a passing acquaintance of Klein's in the days of Studio 54. Early in his career, while working for designer Cathy Hardwick, Ford dreamt of landing a job designing for Calvin Klein. After nine interviews, two with the designer himself, he was offered a job for a small salary. Though he tried to negotiate, no one returned Ford's calls, and he went to work for Marc Jacobs at Perry Ellis and was on the path to fashion stardom at Gucci.

Maurizio Romiti's HdP, owner of Valentino and Fila Sportswear, was in a situation similar to Warnaco's. The company's GFT division was the licensee for Klein's men's tailored clothing sold under the Calvin Klein and cK labels and, as such, would save a bundle on royalty fees, though not nearly as much as Warnaco would. The company, backed by Italy's Romiti and Agnelli clans, was in a financial league all its own, with access to more than enough funds to buy Calvin Klein.

While the speed with which deals were being made was dizzying and the financial environment was one that was out of whack with traditional business times, most fashion insiders assumed there was a billion-dollar price tag for the sometimes controversial company.

Warnaco's Wachner and LVMH's Arnault were the first to express an interest in examining the company's "book," a prospectus of sorts that details what exactly buyers would get, including financial statements. Former Calvin Klein executive

Gabriella Forte was mentioned as a possible buyer as well. She was said to be lining up a financial or strategic partner, perhaps even LVMH, to back her.

As 1999 drew to a close, so did the first round of bidding on Calvin Klein, Inc., and the most likely candidate, Linda Wachner, revealed she was not going on to the next round.

"We're not in the bidding," she said at the time, having offered only $600 million for the company. "I think the best thing to say is the bid we sought was not what they wanted. And I think I know the business as good as anyone, since I'm $60 million of their cash flow."

So which company was the leading contender? Surprisingly, it wasn't the usual suspects of LVMH, Gucci, or Prada. Instead of being a European luxury concern, the companies that emerged were, for the most part, Americans. Tommy Hilfiger, Liz Claiborne, Jones Apparel Group, and even financial investor Texas Pacific Group were still thought to be in the running. While it was being widely reported that the Gucci Group was interested, company officials said Gucci never even looked at Calvin Klein. The dark horse in the sale sweeps was HdP, the CEO of which, Maurizio Romiti, has made no bones about wanting to build the company into a fashion conglomerate. Romiti had been seen in the Calvin Klein offices, which led his company to issue a statement regarding its intentions.

"We have been invited to evaluate a possible acquisition or alliance with Calvin Klein," an HdP spokesperson said, "in light of our long-standing business relationship with the US designer."

The problem with conglomerate HdP was that 80 percent of its revenues came from its magazine and newspaper publishing divisions, which included Rizzoli publishing, Italian *Elle,* and Italian newspaper *Corriere della Sera.* Compared to operating fashion brands, these high-profit, relatively low overhead businesses were preferred by the company's share-holders. While Romiti's aspirations to create a luxury con-glomerate were well known, the internal challenge he was facing was equally well known.

As Klein's deadline to cement a deal by the end of the first quarter loomed, HdP grudgingly admitted that it was out. "We are no longer denying reports that we have lost interest," a company spokesperson said. "You could say the idea is at a standstill."

It seemed the only player left in the game was Tommy Hilfiger, an unlikely buyer, to say the least.

Tommy Hilfiger's rise to the top of the clothes pile was another American rags-to-riches story. Hilfiger, one of nine brothers and sisters, first dabbled in fashion as a teenager when he operated a jeans store called People's Place in his hometown of Elmira, in upstate New York. Though the store was known throughout the region, Hilfiger chose to move to New York City, where he met the Murjani brothers, makers of Gloria Vanderbilt designer jeans. They set him up in a small business making menswear items, and eventually Hil-figer hooked up with businessmen Silas Chou and Lawrence Stroll, who helped grow the business into one of the top designer sportswear collections sold in department stores, expanding far beyond menswear.

The fashion company was one of the first to tap into the public markets, making its initial public offering in 1992. Since that time, Hilfiger has been growing in answer to investors' continuous requests for return.

"My company reached a level of success that certainly surprised me," the designer explained. "However, I faced many different challenges as a result of that. One of them was appealing to Wall Street's continued desire to see me grow."

While Hilfiger's company was growing by more than

$100 million annually, share price wasn't reacting. The company needed to take a more drastic step.

"One alternative that kept coming up was doing an acquisition," the designer said. Hilfiger looked at the companies that were mentioned in mergers and acquisitions circles at the time—North Face, Brooks Brothers, and Valentino—but "none of them was substantial enough to give the growth that we would need to move our $2 billion machine forward."

Calvin Klein, however, offered Hilfiger something that probably would move the machine forward. "We were convinced that if we bought the whole thing—the Warnaco businesses from Warnaco and the Calvin businesses from Calvin," the designer said, the company's stock would feel the bounce.

Negotiations progressed between the Hilfiger camp, Klein executives, and Warnaco's Linda Wachner, but resolving the price issue was a huge problem.

"It was difficult to come to terms with Warnaco on a price, because it was having a difficult time . . . obviously, they were not easy people to deal with," Hilfiger said, referring to the famously difficult Wachner. "And at the same time, Calvin's price was pie in the sky," and the Hilfiger offer was in the range of *only* $850 million.

"We looked at it many, many different ways," Hilfiger recalled, with options being buying just CKI or just Warnaco's jeans and underwear business. "Bottom line, when we took all the different options to my board of directors, they deemed the deal to be nonaccretive. They looked at it as a risk."

In retrospect, Hilfiger still believes it was the right thing to do.

The failure of a deal to materialize from outside buyers

put Warnaco's Linda Wachner in the driver's seat if Klein and Schwartz were still interested in selling the company to her.

The duo from the Bronx, however, realized it was Warnaco, and Wachner in particular, that was standing in the way of a sale. They unceremoniously pulled the company off the block.

"When we matched the offers we received against our own ability to grow the business and ensure the integrity of the brand on our own," Klein and Schwartz said in a joint statement, "we determined that our current positioning enables us most effectively to capitalize in the extraordinary opportunities before us."

One analyst summed up the problem. The buyer "would be buying a royalty stream with little or no control," the biggest part of which Wachner controlled.

Schwartz later summed up what he learned from the exercise to *WWD*. "I don't think anybody would have bought the company for a fair price with Linda Wachner there. No one wanted to be her partner," least of all the duo from the Bronx.

The War with Wachner

C alvin Klein and Barry Schwartz knew they had a problem with Warnaco's Linda Wachner long before they tried to sell Calvin Klein, Inc. However, the reality check they received from putting their company on the market put it into perspective.

Wachner's actions in selling to warehouse clubs and other "gray market," or off-price, retailers had taken the company from a premier designer brand to one that luxury conglomerates would not even look at. Her actions had devalued the brand and got in the way of Klein and Schwartz's big payday. The duo from the Bronx had no choice but to take a decisive step that ultimately would make Wachner pay for her actions.

On May 30, 2000, Calvin Klein, Inc., and its trademark trust filed suit against Linda Wachner, Warnaco, and its various subdivisions in U.S. District Court for the Southern District of New York. The company specifically sued for trademark violations and breach of fiduciary duty and contracts. The charges ranged from Warnaco selling jeans to retailers not approved by Calvin Klein to changing the designs of the jeans after they'd been approved by the designer. Calvin Klein, Inc., was seeking to end its dealings with Warnaco. It wanted the spoils from the improper sales and it wanted damages.

The street-savvy duo's action was quick and bloodless, and they meant business. They even took the unorthodox approach of alerting reporters from *WWD* and the *Wall Street Journal* about the suit prior to serving court documents at Wachner's office. That step was an effort to ensure that she would pay attention to their action, as she hadn't paid attention to the 94 letters Klein and Schwartz had sent in the previous year asking her to stop selling to the off-price retailers.

Wachner's first inkling of trouble came when her assistant interrupted a meeting for the junior women's line at 205 West 39th Street. A *Wall Street Journal* reporter had asked to be patched through to her. "What lawsuit?" she screeched into her mobile phone when the reporter questioned her about the suit.

The first shot had been fired in what was to be the nastiest, bloodiest battle the fashion industry had seen.

The suit itself was substantial, going into great detail listing grievances, and the brutal tone was established early.

"Warnaco and Wachner herself have become a cancer on the value and integrity of the marks," the suit said on its first page, striking a personal note. It wasn't that the duo didn't like Wachner; her actions personally affected them because of the vast amounts of money involved. She was negatively impacting their life's work. "Even though Wachner's abusive and unprofessional management style has, itself, been a major factor in Warnaco's misconduct, Wachner has repeatedly pledged to CKI—and to the public—that Warnaco will honor its obligations and act so as to maintain the long-term value and quality of the marks."

Topping the list of grievances was Wachner and Warnaco's dealings with off-price warehouse retailers like Costco, Sam's Club, and BJ's. The involvement of Costco, in particular, was a problem for Klein, as his company had sued the retailer years prior for allegedly selling counterfeit merchandise.

The suit charged that Warnaco was selling regular first-quality goods to these off-pricers, instead of closeouts and irregular merchandise. In doing so, Warnaco was treating these retailers the same as it would a full-priced merchant like Bloomingdale's or Nordstrom, even offering them "special-cuts," or current-season product made to order. The company's actions were sacrificing cachet for mass-generated cash.

The JC Penney issue was cited in the suit, which said that Wachner told Calvin Klein she wouldn't sell jeanswear and underwear to the moderate department store and then did exactly that.

The suit also charged that Warnaco sold non–Calvin Klein merchandise in its Calvin Klein outlet stores, specifically Chaps Ralph Lauren product, and cited examples seen in outlet stores from Maine to California.

In addition, Warnaco made unapproved changes to designs and "injected" additional items the designers at Calvin Klein had never seen, let alone approved, the suit said. For a designer who dictated what kind of paper clips were used at his company, injecting designs he had not seen was beyond comprehension.

"Warnaco breached its fiduciary duty by misrepresentation, self-dealing and malfeasance," putting short-term financial gain before long-term integrity of the brand, the company said.

"Over the past 30 years, this company has built and nurtured what is recognized as one of the most powerful and successful brands in the world," Klein and Schwartz said. "Warnaco is threatening to erode the Calvin Klein jeanswear and underwear lines through a flood of discounting and other unauthorized sales and practices. . . . Moreover, Warnaco has engaged in a pattern of intentionally deceptive business practices designed to conceal these violations.

"We cannot allow Warnaco's desperate search for short-term revenues to harm CKI brands, nor can we tolerate the repeated and willful violations of our agreements with Warnaco," the duo went on. "Having repeatedly sought to prevent violations of our agreements cooperatively through multiple discussions and letters, and given the recent accelerated decline of Warnaco's business practices, we are left with no choice but to file this suit if we are to preserve the integrity, value and prestige of the Calvin Klein underwear and jeanswear brands."

Wachner claimed to be shocked at the suit. She believed Klein and Schwartz were getting back at her for not being able to cash out.

"Having tried and failed to sell to a number of third parties, including us, why did they adopt this tactic?" she asked, attempting to play the role of victim in the drama.

In preparation for the fight of their careers, Klein and Schwartz had covertly hired attorney David Boies, of the firm Boies, Schiller & Flexner, months before, in January, for a flat fee of $15 million. Boies, a physically unassuming man known for wearing ratty tennis sneakers in the courtroom, later would be known for his representation of presidential contender Al Gore in his failed challenge of the Florida election results. Boies's firm also represented the U.S. Justice

Department in its landmark and successful antitrust case against Microsoft.

"This is a difficult and painful moment," Klein said at the time. He also charged that what Warnaco and Wachner were doing with the jeanswear designs was the equivalent of legal counterfeiting.

However difficult it was, it wasn't bad enough for the inherently shy Klein to avoid the media. Instead, the designer chose to air his dirty laundry on CNN's *Larry King Live.*

In a move that didn't seem to be fully thought out, Klein appeared on the show to discuss a number of things, including the lawsuit.

"Repeatedly over the past three years," Klein said, "we have tried everything possible to rectify the problems that we've had with this company, in the way they manufacture the product, in the quality of the product. It's not up to standard. It's being compromised.

"I've sat with her, my partner has sat with her, the three of us have talked and we have been lied to, and we have been told these things will be taken care of.

"It's my job to protect the trademark, to protect the designs," and, he added, "to protect the brand. It's important that when the consumer buy(s) any of the jeanswear product, that they know that it is our design."

When King asked whether the Calvin Klein jeans that had been on the market in the previous years were his design, he admitted they weren't. In that one statement, Klein eroded customer confidence in his brand of jeans, and, while he came across as a victim on television, painting Wachner as the big bad wolf, seeds of doubt had been planted in many consumers' minds.

"Every time he goes for publicity, he's affirming his business is in trouble," Donny Deutsch, chairman of the Deutsch,

Inc., ad agency, told *WWD* at the time. "If he believes the company with his name is not being run right, taking it public makes him look foolish."

Wachner, on the other hand, did not use the media to strike back, choosing instead to issue a generic statement to anyone who asked while her company strung together its countersuit.

"The complaint is without merit and we are confident that it will be clearly shown to be just that in court," the statement said. "In our view, it's a desperate attempt by Calvin Klein to cover up and distract focus from the highly deteriorated business state of CKI. Throwing stones at Warnaco is not the answer to CKI's problems, Calvin's failed sale of CKI or the positions Calvin Klein or CKI are in today."

While the charges Klein lobbed at Wachner and Warnaco were bad, those she fired back were much more damning.

Wachner hired high-powered counselors at the Williams & Connolly law firm, defenders of former president Bill Clinton in his failed bid to avoid impeachment. The firm left no stone unturned in the countersuit filed by the executive and her company in late June 2000; in fact, it was downright dirty.

Wachner, who herself was not known for her attendance at Calvin Klein product meetings, painted Klein as an absentee landlord.

"CKI has abdicated its responsibilities to design salable products. Mr. Klein apparently no longer had personal involvement in the design of the products that bear his name," the countersuit said. "Since September 1999, Mr. Klein has had no visible or apparent personal involvement in the design of Calvin Klein jeanswear or underwear."

Warnaco cited its problems with the advertising it paid

for, spending 3 percent of gross jeanswear sales. "CKI has compounded its design failures and inadequacies by producing brand advertising that is completely out of touch with the American consumer. . . . For example, as early as 1995, CKI launched an offensive underwear advertisement campaign without Warnaco's approval, which was required under the Administration Agreement," the countersuit said, referring to the ad showing Joel West with legs splayed.

"That particular advertising campaign came only months after another tasteless CKI advertising campaign that actually triggered a Justice Department investigation. . . . Mr. Klein's insistence on producing controversial rather than effective advertising has impaired Warnaco's ability to market Calvin Klein products and, in particular, has damaged Warnaco's ability to build a children's underwear business," the suit said, referring to the scrapped kids-in-underwear campaign from 1999.

The countersuit charged that Klein's appearance on *Larry King Live* resulted in the loss of sales, as his statements damaged the brand. A "customer in Venezuela cited Mr. Klein's statements on *Larry King Live* when it informed Warnaco that it was reducing actual and planned orders for $1.5 million of Warnaco products to $350,000 of Warnaco products." And it charged that Klein "uttered all of these statements with actual malice."

Though she talked tough through her company's charges in the countersuit, shares in Wachner's company were being crushed by the news. In July 2000, she issued a warning that earnings for the year would be between 26 and 36 cents a share, instead of the $1.74 expected by analysts, because of poor sales and costs related to the Calvin Klein litigation. The downgrade led the company's shares to nosedive, dropping 27 percent, or $1.81, to close at $4.94. It was the company's lowest close in a decade.

As the months went by, getting closer to the scheduled court date of January 22, 2001, Judge Jed S. Rakoff issued rulings on motions made on the original suit and counter-suit.

In early August, the judge, small in size and known for his affection for precise documentation, granted a motion that dismissed Wachner personally from four counts of the complaint, saying the Klein suit contained "disguised name calling," when it referred to Wachner.

"What we have here is a contract dispute, a bitter, I'm sorry to say, private dispute," Judge Rakoff said.

In October, the court ruled that nine of Warnaco's 10 counterclaims could be heard.

As the suits wound through pretrial motions, it seemed as though Wachner was edging ahead of Klein. However, Warnaco's earnings and share price were taking a beating, sliding south with each successive negative story about Wachner or Warnaco.

In fact, Calvin Klein, Inc., used Warnaco's lagging sales and mounting debt to take another stab at ending the War-naco licenses. The licensing agreement between Calvin Klein, Inc., and Warnaco for jeanswear specified that the debt-to-equity ratio had to be lower than 5 to 1. In early January 2001, Klein filed a separate suit in New York State Supreme Court to end the license because Warnaco's debt-to-equity ratio exceeded 5 to 1.

Finally, it was time for Warnaco's Linda Wachner and Calvin Klein, Inc.'s Calvin Klein to have their day Manhattan federal court. By 9 A.M. on January 22, 2001, the courtroom on Pearl Street was packed with representatives from every media outlet in town.

In the courtroom, the Klein and Wachner sides were reflective of their very different lifestyles.

Klein was accompanied by longtime friends and family.

Daughter Marci, her new husband Scott Murphy, partner Barry Schwarz and his wife Sheryl, and conversationalist Fran Lebowitz, an old Studio 54 cohort, accompanied Klein.

Wachner, conversely, was all business, joined by her company's internal counsel, her stalwart sidekick Stanley Silverstein, and PR spin doctor Howard Rubenstein.

All of the ugliness that had accumulated for months was concentrated in that tension-packed room. And when Judge Rakoff entered the room to preside, he announced the two warring sides had reached a settlement. In one moment, eight months of sniping came to an anticlimactic end.

"My law clerks are devastated," Rakoff said in a deadpan tone, when he announced the deal.

At this point, the deal was literally sealed with a kiss, albeit a fashionista air kiss, as Calvin crossed over to Wachner's side, shaking her hand and touching cheeks.

"The parties believe their resolution will protect and promote the integrity and success of the Calvin Klein brand for their mutual benefit and the benefit of other Calvin Klein licensees," Klein and Wachner said in a joint statement that was read to the media in the courtroom.

"The parties look forward to expanding jeanswear sale consistent with the image and prestige of Calvin Klein products."

The confidential settlement appeared to leave the arrangement status quo. However, behind-the-scenes sources detailed that although Warnaco got to keep the Calvin Klein jeanswear license, Klein retained firm control over product design and distribution, cutting the number of doors, discount chains in particular, Warnaco could sell to.

The straw that broke the camel's back during settlement talks was a Chaps Ralph Lauren shirt, a fashion insider said. Overruns of the shirt, also manufactured by Warnaco through a license, were relabeled "Calvin Klein," without the designer's knowledge. When presented with this physical evidence, Wachner started to deal.

While industry watchers were split between whether Warnaco or Calvin Klein was the winner, history has shown that Warnaco and Linda Wachner ultimately paid the price. Her company filed for Chapter 11 bankruptcy protection in May 2001, and Wachner was dethroned as chairman and CEO a scant five months later.

With Klein released from the constraints of the legal proceedings against Wachner and Warnaco, he got on with the business of Calvin Klein, Inc. But the lessons learned from the lawsuits were costly—the two companies are linked for good times and bad. Warnaco is a cross Calvin Klein has to bear until 2044, unless the licenses are sold or are somehow returned to Calvin Klein, Inc.

CHAPTER 15

Streamlining for Success

The settlement of their case with Warnaco allowed Klein and Schwartz to refocus on the business at hand in the house of Klein.

However, after all the tumult, many fashion watchers believed the partners had missed their opportunity to hit the big time and that the brand was twisting in the wind, with very few places to go. It didn't help that the velvet curtain that hid all the truths about who manufactured Calvin Klein merchandise had been pulled back over and over again through the Warnaco suit and the press that surrounded it. Now that consumers knew Calvin Klein wasn't actually making the jeans they wore, would they still want to buy them and other Klein products? The brand had taken a massive blow.

Klein's big Asian initiative, Calvin Klein Japan, had already imploded, with the partnership being dissolved at the end of 1999. Klein, unhappy with the progress the partnership was making, wanted to assert more control over the licensees there.

While former executive Gabriella Forte worked tirelessly to make Calvin Klein an international brand, many of the deals she put in place had fallen apart or were starting to fall apart by early 2001.

The enormous Stefanel joint venture was terminated by both partners in March 2001 because it failed to produce the kinds of results both Stefanel and Klein wanted. The cK Calvin Klein sportswear collection failed to have the kind of draw in Europe that both parties initially expected, and the ambitious plans for store openings were slowed by a lack of customers. The project was a money drain for Stefanel.

The company's license with Mariella Burani was the next to go. Klein and Schwartz actually bought back the license to manufacture the company's top-end collection, which had three years remaining.

To one former insider, the ending of these agreements was expected and almost too long in coming. "All the licenses Gabriella Forte set up for Calvin . . . there was no logistical organization on his side, and he didn't care." The insider added, "They're all gone, and I think the truth of the matter is [the brand] lost the panache."

There was industry buzz about Klein negotiating with Italian media and fashion concern HdP to take over these businesses. However, in March 2001, Maurizio Romiti once again affirmed that the company was still concentrating its efforts in the media sector.

"Over the next three years, we are committing ourselves to the development of the editorial and communications sectors," Romiti said at the time. "We are rapidly expanding both our traditional editorial activities and our multimedia business in Europe."

Later that spring, Klein's streamlining strategy was made

obviously apparent when he discontinued the cK Calvin Klein bridge sportswear line in the United States, slashing more than 90 jobs from his company's headquarters.

One main reason for the elimination was the designer's growing disenchantment with the bridge area in the American department stores he had once been so hot to sell. "If you look at cK around the world, [it] is a young collection that sits beautifully with the cK Calvin Klein jeans collection," Klein said. "In the US, where it is carried in department stores in the bridge department," without the denim collection, "it's just not a fit for us."

Instead of accepting the cutbacks as a negative, Klein spun it into a positive "restructuring" of the company. Klein and Schwartz would be concentrating their efforts on the high-end collection. The business was going back to its original roots. While it operated at a financial loss, its presence and positioning served as a calling card for the brand, as did the company's own stores.

"The collection is what sets the tone for everything," Klein said at the time.

The strategy to grow the collection involved opening flagship stores across the world in some 20 cities to supplement the company's current flagships in New York City, Dallas, and Tokyo (a new Paris flagship would open in March 2002). Klein set his sights on cities such as Los Angeles, San Francisco, Chicago, Houston, London, and Milan.

"We want to open retail stores to focus on and supplement our men's and women's collection business," the designer said. "Freestanding stores are an investment, but you get a return on your investment. When you tie it all together, sales increase."

The dramatic cuts and shuffling of executives made many fashion watchers believe the business was going to be closed. Rumors ran rampant that the entire American business was going to be shuttered and that new headquarters were being established in Milan to keep a watch on the company's licensing efforts.

In June 2001, Calvin Klein was honored with the Council of Fashion Designers of America's Lifetime Achievement Award. It was somewhat ironic that his peers chose this time to honor his lifework, particularly since he was gearing down his business. Also, the fact that he'd been in business for almost 35 years, longer than probably 80 percent of all fashion companies, made it surprising that Klein wasn't honored earlier in his career.

"I don't feel this sense of 'life achievement,' " the designer told *WWD* at the time. "While I recognize that we've managed to do a few good things, I'm still looking at how to do it all better, and how we get to the next place."

Klein attended the awards with his estranged wife Kelly and stalwart friend Fran Lebowitz in tow. With all three dressed from head to toe in Calvin Klein, the trio was shocked when they were splattered with tofu-cream pies while walking the red carpet.

The attack was not payback for that first licensing deal with Alixandre for fur coats 30 years earlier, but simply an accident. Klein and company just happened to get in the way of a People for the Ethical Treatment of Animals (PETA) protester as she attempted to pelt Teutonic terror and Chanel designer, Karl Lagerfeld, with the pies. Though slightly soiled by the attack, Klein pulled it together to accept the award from *Interview* magazine editor and longtime friend Ingrid Sischy.

"It is as impossible to conceive of fashion without Calvin Klein, as it would be to imagine the New York Harbor without the Statue of Liberty," Sischy said in her introduction. Klein, she added, "has hit the Zeitgeist on the head more times than Madonna," obviously having better aim than the PETA protester.

While Calvin Klein sharpened his focus on his high-end collection, his partner and former nemesis Linda Wachner was fighting to keep her company afloat. Already suffering from the ill effects of events ranging from lagging retail sales to skyrocketing interest charges and debt payments, the negative publicity and legal fees related to the Calvin Klein suit tipped the scales in the direction of a Chapter 11 bankruptcy filing.

With more than $2.5 billion in debt, Wachner performed a juggling act every day in the spring of 2001, trying to keep everybody paid and happy. Earlier, she had rolled all the company's debt into one big financing package shared by 17 banks, but still hadn't finalized all the details on the deal seven months later. In both April and May, she faced deadlines to finalize the loans, but in each instance obtained 30-day waivers, allowing her to push her D day until June.

Certainly, the stagnant retail environment was working against Wachner. Warnaco couldn't make a profit from retail partners that were constantly slashing prices and profit margins or going out of business altogether in a post-Internet economy that was dipping into a recession. It didn't help that the Warnaco brands were quickly losing luster as they were sold through more and more mass channels.

On June 11, Warnaco finally had to face its reality and filed for Chapter 11 bankruptcy. The move put all of the company's licenses potentially up for grabs, as every deal is basically rendered null when a filing occurs. Warnaco would later have to petition bankruptcy court for the agreements to be affirmed on the grounds they were required for the business to go on.

However, Klein and Schwartz were keeping a close watch on the situation, as they were interested in buying back their underwear business and the jeanswear license if at all possible. As the two businesses would easily carry a $500 million price tag, it was thought the duo would tap an outside partner to make the purchase.

Linda Wachner, on the other hand, was fighting for her life, trying unsuccessfully to keep her job. The decision came down to former American Express CEO Harvey Golub, a member of Warnaco's board handpicked by Wachner. As chair of the company's restructuring committee, he determined there was no way she could stay on at the company. After a 12-hour meeting in which the board tried unsuccessfully to sew up a deal for her to resign gracefully, the board ousted Wachner without severance, which she later sued for, ultimately getting less than 10 percent of what she asked for.

The company named turnaround specialist Antonio Alvarez as the new CEO, and he quickly set a new tone for Warnaco's business, putting six of the company's divisions on the block. The remaining divisions, which included Calvin Klein jeanswear and underwear, he added, could be bought for the right price.

"When you're in Chapter 11, you're always open and are going to listen to those who come to you," he said.

CHAPTER 16

Phillips-Van Who?

Linda Wachner's ouster and the admission that Warnaco's brands were up for grabs unleashed a feeding frenzy among companies that were in a position to make acquisitions.

VF Corporation, Phillips-Van Heusen, Warren Buffett's Berkshire Hathaway, and, of course, Calvin Klein, Inc., were mentioned as potential bidders for some or all of the bankrupt company's pieces. Tommy Hilfiger even reemerged as a potential buyer for the Calvin Klein underwear and jeanswear businesses.

In the aftermath of the high-glamour conglomerates and status-chasing stockholders, the new era would be defined by value. The new millennium brought with it baggage from the end of the previous century, most notably a financial hangover caused by the bust of the Internet boom. The millions of dollars Internet-based businesses pumped into the markets were gone and investors were faced with the real-ization many tech-sector stock options weren't worth the paper they were printed on. The entire economy, already suffering from these setbacks, was affected further by the uncertainties unleashed by the terror attacks of September 11, 2001. Consumers, concerned about the weak economy and unemployment, looked for value when making pur-chases.

Retailers like Target, Wal-Mart, Kohl's, and even the ware-house clubs benefited from the downturn in the economy. And these store chains looked for ways to retain their new-found customers.

In the field of mass merchants, Target stood out because it realized value-priced merchandise didn't have to be ugly or bland. In its aim to bring class to the masses, Target con-tracted with well-known designers to create exclusive col-lections for its stores. Its first major success came with a designer named Mossimo Gianulli.

The designer's namesake company had one of the hottest fashion IPOs in the mid-1990s, but had fallen on hard times and had filed for Chapter 11 bankruptcy protection. Gian-ulli's deal with Target paid the designer a multi-million-dollar licensing fee that allowed him to salvage his name and company and at the same time sell thousands of gar-ments for young men and women, most priced under $29.99.

European retailers H&M and Zara also burst onto the scene in this time period, with their runway knockoffs hit-ting the market faster than the designer's products that inspired them.

Consumers were being retrained to believe that they didn't have to spend beaucoup bucks on designer labels like Michael Kors, Gucci, and Calvin Klein when they could get the same looks from H&M for under $100. And if they did splurge on an expensive designer garment, pairing it with a $12.99 Mossimo T-shirt was perfectly acceptable, even admirable.

In addition, publicly held companies that catered to the middle—the Jones Apparel Group, Liz Claiborne, Kellwood, Phillips-Van Heusen, and the like—benefited. These companies showed that there was not only big business in the middle price range, but there were also decent profits to be had.

Phillips-Van Heusen (PVH) had expressed an interest in buying Calvin Klein, Inc., when the company was for sale in 1999. While Calvin Klein and Barry Schwartz didn't say no to any prospective buyer, they were more interested in focusing on the luxury players.

"I met Bruce Klatsky [PVH's chairman and CEO] a few years ago," Schwartz told *WWD*. "The first time around, he was very interested in buying the company. We didn't feel he had the credentials the others had," or pockets as deep.

Unbeknownst to Klein and Schwartz, Phillips-Van Heusen had credentials that stretched illustriously over the past century.

Polish immigrant Moses Phillips started his business in 1881 selling flannel shirts to coal miners from a pushcart. After upgrading to a horse and buggy, he founded the Phillips-Jones Corporation in 1907. As the company passed from Moses to subsequent generations of Phillips, it grew into a maker of dress shirts with semisoft collars patented by the Van Heusen Company, which was eventually acquired by Phillips-Jones and renamed Phillips-Van Heusen in 1957.

The Van Heusen label became a household name in the 1950s when the company used actors Anthony Quinn, Burt

Lancaster, and Ronald Reagan in advertising its Century shirts, which "won't wrinkle ever," the company's ads claimed.

PVH was a family-run business until 1993, when it named Klatsky chairman and chief executive officer. Under his tenure, the company diversified its product offerings for brands Van Heusen, Izod, and GH Bass, as well as licensed product for Geoffrey Beene, Arrow, DKNY, and Kenneth Cole.

Interestingly, PVH made a concerted effort in the 1980s to stop doing business with stores and distributors that allowed PVH merchandise to reach cut-rate vendors, something that must have appealed to Klein and Schwartz.

While PVH did not make the final cut of prospective buyers in 2000, Klein, Schwartz, and Klatsky kept in contact, which resulted in the company being awarded Calvin Klein's dress shirt license in 2002.

The launch of the cK Calvin Klein dress shirts in fall 2002 was the most successful launch PVH had ever had, which fueled Klatsky and company president Mark Weber to get on with the deal to buy the house of Klein.

While the parties had kept their negotiations under the radar, the intensifying talks leaked out once their respective bankers, lawyers, and other affiliated consultants got involved.

PVH partnered with Apax Partners, an international private equity group with over $11 billion in assets, which was led by general partner David Landau.

Instead of hiring Lazard Freres, as they had the first time the company was on the block, Klein and Schwartz chose to work with an adviser with whom they had a closer personal relationship.

The duo first met Stormy Byorum when she was managing director at Citibank. The banker, named after the bad Texas weather she was born into, negotiated the duo's $58 million loan in 1993 that enabled them to pay back David Geffen's personal bailout.

Byorum subsequently became friendly with Klein and Schwartz and eventually became good friends with fellow horse aficionado Kelly Klein. In 1990, Kelly Klein and Byorum purchased Wild Ocean Farms, a 30-acre equestrian estate with both indoor and outdoor riding areas in Bridgehampton, New York, to house their 10 show horses.

Though her firm, Violy, Byorum & Partners, specialized in Latin American deals, her personal relationship with Kelly and history with Klein and Schwartz gave Byorum the inside track for the Calvin Klein job.

As usually is the case, the moment there was a hint of a deal on Seventh Avenue, the usual European suspects were trotted out as potential buyers, though the only deals the luxury conglomerates were doing in that period were selling some of their own divisions.

PVH was clearly the front-runner in the negotiations with Calvin Klein. While he wouldn't come out and specifically say it, Emanuel Chirico, PVH's chief financial officer, hinted that the company would be making an acquisition when he spoke on the company's conference call to discuss its third-quarter earnings with financial analysts who followed the company for investors.

"We would be willing in the short term to take on some extra leverage," Chirico said, "to do the right strategic acquisition, especially one that could transform us."

Once it became apparent there was a deal to be done, others—mainly the VF Corporation—did look at buying the company.

As a manufacturer of underwear and jeans, VF Corporation seemed to be the most well-suited partner Klein and Schwartz could ask for, particularly if the company would be interested in buying Warnaco's portions of the Calvin Klein business.

VF Corporation became aggressively involved in the bidding for Calvin Klein, assuming that the company would be able to purchase the designer's pieces from Warnaco, still operating under Chapter 11 bankruptcy protection.

However, Warnaco was not interested in selling. The jeans-and-panty maker was one month away from emerging from bankruptcy and wanted to stay on track. "We are continuing to pursue our stand-alone plan of reorganization and expect to emerge in early 2003," said a Warnaco spokesman.

Since VF wanted all or nothing, it backed out, leaving Klein, Schwartz, and their advisers to work a deal with PVH. And a deal was going to get done if Klein had his way.

Once again, getting paid was in the forefront of the designer's mind. Klein had watched his peers Ralph Lauren, Tommy Hilfiger, and Donna Karan all receive huge paydays when their companies made initial public offerings. Donna Karan received a second windfall for her trademarks and her portion of Donna Karan, International when it was all sold to Bernard Arnault's LVMH in 2000. Klein had waited long enough for his piece of the pie, even though he earned $21.5 million in 2000 and an estimated $30 million in 2001. His time had come.

On the morning of December 17, 2002, PVH announced it was in discussions to acquire Calvin Klein, Inc. And at the close of the market that day, the company issued another announcement—"Phillips-Van Heusen to acquire Calvin Klein for $700 million."

In return for the brand name, the collection business, and the brand's related licensing revenue, Klein and Schwartz received $400 million in cash and approximately $30 million in PVH stock. In addition, Klein received warrants and ongoing financial incentives that could add up to another $300 million.

"This is, without a doubt the greatest day of my business career," Klatsky said during the company's conference call for analysts. "We have felt over the past three years that we basically had all of the pistons working . . . but that to give us top-line revenue growth, we needed to make an acquisition of some consequence that would take us into the years ahead. We wanted to buy a great brand and that's exactly what we did," Klatsky said.

PVH purchased Calvin Klein for the same reasons Tommy Hilfiger cited as the reason it was looking at the acquisition three years before—top-line growth. However, PVH believed it could grow the brand's business worldwide and at different price levels, while Hilfiger bowed out.

"We've already begun plans to launch a men's sportswear collection. We are presently in conversations with a number of the larger women's apparel companies," Klatsky continued, "to launch a major women's sportswear effort. Those will be our primary two initiatives.

"This is what we've been looking for. This is the growth engine for the future of our company. We're going to do it cautiously, we're going to do it carefully, and we're going to preserve the integrity and the positioning of the Calvin Klein brand."

Klein seemed relieved that he and Schwartz had found what they believed was the right buyer. "Barry and I have talked to a number of different companies over these last few years," Klein said. "Until Bruce came to speak to Barry about two years ago . . . until we really started to get to know each other, I never felt the chemistry was right with anyone and I vetoed every possibility up until now."

Schwartz agreed: "We were in total agreement on selling

the company. I think Phillips-Van Heusen will be very good for the brand. If you look back, we built an incredible brand, starting with virtually nothing. I think the name is known worldwide," he said. "I think they can take it to the next level."

Calvin Klein had finally gotten what he wanted—a payday that gave him the freedom to do as he pleased.

CHAPTER 17

Tomorrow

C alvin Klein is 61 years old (as of press date), and has been operating his business for more than 35 years. With daughter Marci an established television producer and no well-known design partner to succeed Klein at the top of the empire, it is unclear what exactly will happen to the creative direction of the company under new owners Phillips-Van Heusen.

The precedent for fashion houses living beyond the namesake designer is firmly established in Europe. Chanel, Pierre Balmain, Givenchy, Gucci, and Christian Dior are just a few the brands that have continued on to new successes well beyond the lives of their namesake designers. Luxury conglomerates like the Gucci Group or Bernard Arnault's LVMH Moet Hennessy Louis Vuitton have built vast empires by revitalizing brands like these old gems.

American fashion houses, however, have yet to realize successes like these on any scale. Certainly, the fact that American fashion as we know it has been around only since the second half of the twentieth century plays into this. Designer houses that have lived on despite the death of their namesake designers—brands like Perry Ellis, Anne Klein, and Halston—all exist in the marketplaces of America, yet it is debatable whether a licensed wallet being sold at Marshall's for $8.99 truly represents these designer's visions and denotes the successful continuation of an empire.

The house of the late Bill Blass appeared to be a recent exception to this rule. When the late designer decided to retire for health reasons, Blass, one of the longest-lasting American designers and, in fact, known as the "dean of American fashion," very deliberately sold his company to trusted executives he'd worked with for years. He then worked with the new owners to find a designer who would embody his design philosophy.

After a number of false starts, it seemed the company had found success with Scandinavian designer Lars Nilsson, who lasted longer than all of the other designers. However, Nilsson was unceremoniously let go in February 2003, the day after his fall 2003 fashion show in the tents in New York's fashion week, with his replacement, Michael Vollbracht, waiting in the wings.

PVH has lofty aspirations for the brand of Calvin Klein. When the acquisition was announced, the company made clear the areas it believes it can expand—"better men's and women's sportswear and accessories lines; global expansion through . . . licensing partners; global expansion through Calvin Klein retail stores; and taking advantage of additional growth opportunities in Europe and Asia."

The company hit the ground running, announcing its first strategic partnership with Italian suit-maker Vestimenta to manufacture the Calvin Klein men's and women's designer collections a mere two weeks after the Calvin Klein acquisition was completed. The deal marks the end of Calvin Klein,

Inc., as a manufacturer, as the designer collection, a money loser for ages, was the only component that the company didn't license out. As with most of the other agreements, Calvin Klein, Inc., will "retain all responsibilities for design, marketing, advertising and public relations, as well as control over distribution."

It is interesting to note that PVH reiterates that the "design of the apparel collections would be retained by Calvin Klein, Inc. as well as management of the strategic partnership with Vestimenta." It spells out that Tom Murry, president and COO of Calvin Klein, will have the final say, with no mention of what the designer himself will contribute.

This comes on the heels of speculation that the designer's collection that was shown on Valentine's Day, 2003 will be his last. With hundreds of fashion reporters, buyers, and special guests—including Renée Zellweger, Calvin Klein Crave model Travis, and Hillary Swank and husband Chad Lowe—in the audience, Klein lingered a bit on the runway when he came out for his bow. What is normally a quick walk-and-wave routine was replaced by a stroll with a long pause, as he appeared reticent to turn around and leave the stage he has occupied for so many years.

Unbeknownst to most in the audience, an internal memo had been circulated to the top brass at Calvin Klein, Inc., that day formalizing Klein's role as "consulting creative director" to Calvin Klein, Inc., under PVH's ownership. This came on the heels of partner Barry Schwartz's retirement, which became official when the PVH deal closed on February 12, 2003.

Being true to his first love, Schwartz was leaving to devote his time to the horse-racing tracks. The former chairman and CEO of Calvin Klein, Inc., was named chairman of the board for the New York Racing Association in October 2000. Instead of devoting only half of his time to overseeing the Saratoga, Belmont, and Aqueduct tracks, he could immerse himself in the unpaid position.

However, the language in PVH's filings with the Securities and Exchange Commission dictated this day would come. In the details released when the deal was agreed upon, specifics about Klein and Schwartz's noncompete agreements and eligibility for health coverage under COBRA, which is de rigueur for former employees, were outlined. In addition, a figurative eviction notice was served on the duo.

"PVH agrees that it will maintain and make available . . . to Mr. Klein and Mr. Schwartz, their existing office space for the benefit of each Mr. Klein and Mr. Schwartz on an as-needed basis and for transition purposes for a period of up to 90 days following the closing."

At the end of May 2003, Calvin Klein could be a man without an office. However, it is debatable whether he will need one.

"I just can't see Calvin doing nothing. But I can't see him showing up there, working 48 weeks a year, nine to nine," a fashion insider said. "The guy is getting $200 million cash. He's 60 years old and he's in fine fettle—how much does he want to do?" the insider asked. "Do you know how much work it takes to put together a collection? He's turned out over 100 collections. How many times can he get his hackles up—get the old fire in the belly?

"At the end of the day, he worked for it. The big question is going to be what does Calvin want to do? He spent his whole life working for an objective . . . to have a wonderful company . . . that appeals to his aesthetic, but also to have the security of knowing that he is set, no matter what. This is not a rehearsal, this is life."

Though Klein did pocket more money in the sale than most will see in a lifetime, there is the potential for much more. The deal to sell the company also included an agreement whereby Klein will receive payments based on sales of all Calvin Klein products through 2018, which leads many to believe the designer will keep a finger in the pot.

Still, Calvin Klein, the person, has quickly faded from the picture at PVH. In its first conference call with stock analysts and the media after the purchase of Calvin Klein, Inc., all that PVH execs said intimated that Klein, once a micromanager, has washed his hands of the whole affair.

"Bruce and myself are currently meeting with all of the licensees over the course of the next 30 to 60 days to make sure we understand their business, to understand where the growth opportunities are," said PVH president Mark Weber, making no mention of the designer acting as conduit.

The company's immediate plans include the launch of a moderately priced men's and women's sportswear collection. One might assume this collection will have a similar kind of appeal to the one the cK collection was supposed to have when it was launched. Or it could have a different scope altogether.

Just who will be responsible for the design of this collection is the big question. Calvin Klein, Inc., has an able design staff, headed by former Gucci designer Francisco Costa. Still, in the past, no matter how much of the collections were designed by his staff, Klein's fingerprints were all over each collection. Without his involvement, one has to wonder just how "Calvin Klein," the moderate-priced collection will be.

Designer Jeffrey Banks believes there is a potential hit in Phillips-Van Heusen's more moderately priced aspirations, "as long as [Calvin Klein] is there and is directing the design room. I think it'll be a total disaster if he's not really involved."

Banks cited Klein's unrivaled taste and knack for being able to see at a glance what works on a garment and what doesn't. "We would do a fitting for a coat . . . with a welt pocket. Calvin could look at it, walking in the door of the fitting room and would say 'the pocket's wrong.' He just has an eye for proportion. When you get into minimalist design, every eighth of an inch counts. And if Calvin's not going to be there, it's not going to work.

"He's the greatest editor in the world," Banks continued. "The best designers are the best editors. The people who can sit there and look at something . . . a dress that's been embroidered and labored over for hundreds of hours, and say, 'You know what? It's wrong. Scrap it. Cut it out of the collection. I don't care how much money we spent on it, I don't care how many hours we labored over it. Cut it.' Calvin could always do that. He was always the most cutthroat with his own line. And that's why his collections look the way they do.

"The customer is much smarter today," Banks said. "They're much more informed. They go on Style.com and know what Michael Kors is doing 10 minutes after Michael Kors does it. You can't fool them, they know the real thing and they want the real thing. They know the difference.

"If he's not going to be involved, it's going to be a disaster," he concluded.

There's always the possibility PVH will bring in another designer to carry the mantle of Calvin Klein. The most obvious choice for this honor would be Narciso Rodriguez, who served on Klein's design staff for years before striking out on his own and carries many of the same sensibilities in his own design.

It is interesting to note that Carolyn Bessette Kennedy, the style icon often cited as the embodiment of the Calvin Klein look, is most often pictured wearing a Narciso Rodriguez–designed gown for her wedding.

Rumors circulated through fashion circles in the days after Klein's last show that Rodriguez was being courted, which top retailers seemed excited about. The designer, however, denied it was happening, saying through his spokesman that he was focusing on his own business.

Still, "I think Narciso is the new Calvin," said a former insider. "I think he does Calvin better than Calvin did Calvin."

Perhaps Calvin Klein Industries said it best in a 1985 filing with the Securities and Exchange Commission (SEC): "There can be no assurance that CKI's present level of sales could be maintained if the personal design and supervisory services of Calvin Klein were no longer available to it."

Epilogue

Calvin's influence on the fashion industry and on society as a whole is palpable in many ways. From the early days when he dominated the designer jeans craze and revolutionized the underwear business to breaking all established rules for fragrance to creating multiple master brands, many will benefit from his actions for years to come.

The ground broken by Calvin Klein's advertising is in another league entirely. The designer can be credited with breaking more barriers than any other when it comes to showing nudity and pushing sex and its various hetero-homo variations into the mainstream for all to deal with. As an advertising pioneer, Klein has paved the way for companies like Guess, Benetton, Kenneth Cole, and French Connection that use provocative images and words to garner attention for their brands.

The Gucci Group's Tom Ford has grown to occupy the advertising space Klein once did in a creative and provocative sense. However, Ford would never have been able to show a naked Sophie Dahl in the Yves Saint Laurent's Opium ad or a model with the Gucci logo shaved into her pubic hair if Klein had not carved the way many years before.

Klein's paradox lies in the fact that he considers his high-end collection his calling card, yet made his name and fortune selling affordable products to the hoi polloi. While he will always be known in certain circles for his modern, clean sportswear that helped establish the American fashion look on a world stage, most will remember him for jeans, underwear, and perfume.

"Calvin's lower-priced business is such a big percent of the total that to sell anything special to special stores is really difficult," one former exec reflected. The high-end products are "not what he is," the exec added, "it *is* who he perceives he is," an inherent irony.

In researching this book, I regularly visited Klein's store in New York and also shopped the store in Paris. On each visit, I was struck by the lack of customers—on many occasions, I was the only customer in the store. Yet everywhere else—in line at a Federal Express counter, in the grocery store, or on an airplane—people were wearing cK Calvin Klein jeans, logo shirts, accessories, and underwear.

"The truth of the matter [is that] it must be very frustrating for Calvin," said a former insider. "He never could really get [the collection] right, but he knew what was right."

The shy boy from Mosholu Parkway never really went away—he was and is still haunting Calvin Klein. The way he operated in his day-to-day workings led many to believe he is still trying to fit in. From his choice of high school and his quest to have the same kind of celebrity Halston had to the way he operated with his employees and even in his personal life, Klein was always that insecure guy trying to fit in through his actions. He never did quite believe in himself, instead surrounding himself with those who were more overtly confident of their talents or supported his.

"In his subconscious, he believes that people are going to realize any minute now that he had been fooling everybody for all these years," said a former insider. "The mask is going to come off and they're going to see him for what he is—this gay kid from the Bronx.

"It's a shame, because he's so hugely talented and he's a really nice person," the former insider said. "He tortures himself with insecurity to a degree that is just unbelievable."

Klein's self-doubt most likely fuels his desire to drink and indulge in recreational drugs, a habit that has tragically resurfaced in Klein's daily life.

The world was clued in that something was amiss with the designer through a bizarre incident at a New York Knicks basketball game on March 24, 2003. In front of thousands of onlookers and many members of the media, Klein wandered from his courtside seat to approach player Latrell Sprewell as the player was about to throw the ball inbounds. Klein put his hand on Sprewell's arm and mumbled something to the stunned player before the wobbly designer was escorted back to his seat by two security guards.

Klein was reportedly drinking that night, and was rumored to be under the influence of other substances as well.

Two weeks later, the designer came clean.

"For many years, I've been able to successfully address my substance abuse issues, which for anyone is a lifelong process, through strict adherence to counseling and regular attendance at meetings," Klein said in a statement. "However, when I recently stopped attending meetings regularly, I suffered a setback. Fortunately, I was lucky with the help of others to recognize the problem. And now, I'm again getting the treatment I need to resume a healthy and productive lifestyle."

His actions and subsequent entry into a rehabilitation program have intensified the interest in what Klein's involvement will be with Calvin Klein, Inc., under the ownership of Phillips-Van Heusen.

As part of the original sale agreement, Klein will receive royalty payments based on the performance of his former company through 2018, so it behooves the designer to keep his image clean. In addition, it is believed the designer has a three-year contract with PVH to work a specified number of days each year providing design direction and making appearances at special events.

However, it has been reported that all is not well between Klein and PVH—that the apparel giant has been disappointed with Klein's initial lack of involvement and that his actions on the basketball court and subsequent announcement about rehab may be damaging to the brand. Regardless, we've certainly not heard the last word on the relationship between Klein and PVH.

While Klein's future involvement with his namesake company is in question, the designer has moved on to other projects. Klein is said to be following in his wife Kelly's footsteps and embarking on a second career as a photographer. He's even rented out photographer Annie Leibovitz's studio on occasion to do test shoots. His talent for recognizing zeitgeist will undoubtedly serve him well as a photographer.

And no matter what, millions of people across the world will wake up tomorrow and dress in clothes that bear his name, making the brand, and his name, as ubiquitous as Coca-Cola.

Notes

Prologue

Page 1 "The reception/benefit . . ." The event described is from the author's own experience and recollection.

Page 3 "The duo originally . . ." Frank DiGiacomo, "Authors Say Geffen, Walters, Putnam Came Between Them and Their Calvin," *New York Observer,* September 27, 1993.

Page 4 "The event was . . ." The event described is from the author's own experience and recollection.

Page 5 "Klein was so . . ." Author's interview, informed source.

Chapter 1

Page 8 "You couldn't avoid . . ." Author's interview.

Page 8 "The subway, up until . . ." Ibid.

Page 8 "Nobody had . . ." Ibid.

Page 8 "It was, to use . . ." Ibid.

Page 9 "It is in this . . ." "Calvin Klein: A Stylish Obsession," *A&E Biography,* 1996.

Page 10 "Calvin and Barry were . . ." Steven Gaines and Sharon Churcher, *Obsession: The Lives and Times of Calvin Klein,* Birch Lane Press, 1994.

Page 10   "It was a time . . ." Author's interview.

Page 11   "These people had more . . ." Ibid.

Page 11   "It was very . . ." Ibid.

Page 12   "He was a very . . ." "Calvin Klein: A Stylish Obsession," *A&E Biography,* 1996.

Page 12   "Everyone used to . . ." Ibid.

Page 13   "The alumni of the school . . ." Author's interview.

Page 13   "That 'made him . . .' " Ibid.

Page 13   "A trip to the Paradise . . ." Ibid.

Page 15   "Like in high school . . ." Steven Gaines and Sharon Churcher, *Obsession: The Lives and Times of Calvin Klein,* Birch Lane Press, 1994.

Chapter 2

Page 16   "I earned $55 . . ." Glenn Plaskin, "Calvin Klein: Playboy Interview," *Playboy,* May 1984.

Page 17   "After World War II . . ." Author's interview.

Page 18   "The elder Millstein . . ." Ibid.

Page 18   "He made his first . . ." Ibid.

Page 19   "I was the first . . ." "Reminiscings: Dan Millstein," *Clothes,* July 1, 1973.

Page 19   "He was one . . ." Author's interview.

Page 20   "I learned a lot . . ." Glenn Plaskin, "Calvin Klein: Playboy Interview," *Playboy,* May 1984.

Page 20   "Calvin wanted to be . . ." Author's interview.

Page 21   "The fashion world . . ." Glenn Plaskin, "Calvin Klein: Playboy Interview," *Playboy,* May 1984.

Page 21   "Millstein made a . . ." Ibid.

Page 22   "When Calvin asked me . . ." Lisa Lockwood, "Bye Bye Barry," *WWD,* February 13, 2003.

Page 22   "I don't want the money . . ." Glenn Plaskin, "Calvin Klein: Playboy Interview," *Playboy,* May 1984.

Page 23   "This is the only . . ." Ibid.

Page 24   "I filled up four . . ." Lisa Lockwood, "Bye Bye Barry," *WWD,* February 13, 2003.

Page 25   "I didn't want to . . ." Glenn Plaskin, "Calvin Klein: Playboy Interview," *Playboy,* May 1984.

Page 25   "Mr. Klein, I will pay you . . ." Ibid.

Page 26   "What impressed me most . . ." Elizabeth Peer with Lisa Whitman, "Stylish Calvinism," *Newsweek,* November 3, 1975.

Page 26 "What's a Bonwit?" "Calvin Klein: A Stylish Obsession," *A&E Biography,* 1996.

Chapter 3

Page 27 "Klein and Schwartz chose . . ." Glenn Plaskin, "Calvin Klein: Playboy Interview," *Playboy,* May 1984.

Page 28 "At the York Hotel," Lisa Lockwood, "Bye Bye Barry," *WWD,* February 13, 2003.

Page 28 "It was seven days a week . . ." Elsa Klensch, "Calvin Klein, and Anti-Materialist Turns 30 and Waits to Go Co-op," *WWD,* 1973.

Page 28 "For Schwartz, the early years . . ." Lisa Lockwood, "Bye Bye Barry," *WWD,* February 13, 2003.

Page 28 "Calvin was doing smart . . ." Author's interview.

Page 31 "He was truly . . ." Steven Gaines and Sharon Churcher, *Obses-sion: The Lives and Times of Calvin Klein,* Birch Lane Press, 1994.

Page 31 "I was asked . . ." Author's interview.

Page 31 "Klein 'accepted . . .' " Ibid.

Page 32 "School said . . ." Ibid.

Page 33 "I want you to . . ." Ibid.

Page 33 "Zack was incredibly talented . . ." Ibid. The proliferation of Scorpios did not stop with Zack Carr and Jeffrey Banks. Calvin Klein, born November 19, and Kelly Rector, born November 2, also shared this sign.

Page 34 "That was his first . . ." Ibid.

Page 35 "I had a friend . . ." Ibid.

Page 36 "All these models . . ." Ibid.

Page 36 "Instead of growing . . ." Steven Gaines and Sharon Churcher, *Obsession: The Lives and Times of Calvin Klein,* Birch Lane Press, 1994.

Page 37 "We used to make . . ." Author's interview.

Page 37 "Without start-up costs . . ." Ibid.

Page 39 "In 1975 . . ." Ibid.

Page 40 "Instead of sending . . ." Ibid.

Page 40 "Needless to say . . ." Multiple sources.

Page 41 "I think we've got . . ." Glenn Plaskin, "Calvin Klein: Playboy Interview," *Playboy,* May 1984.

Page 41 "Before Carl went . . ." Author's interview.

Page 41 "In addition to . . ." Multiple sources.

Page 42   "More than 200,000 . . ." Steven Gaines and Sharon Churcher, *Obsession: The Lives and Times of Calvin Klein,* Birch Lane Press, 1994.

Page 43   "Patti's a really . . ." Glenn Plaskin, "Calvin Klein: Playboy Interview," *Playboy,* May 1984.

Page 44   "Reading is to . . ." Steven Gaines and Sharon Churcher, *Obsession: The Lives and Times of Calvin Klein,* Birch Lane Press, 1994.

Page 44   "In the week following their . . ." "Calvin Klein: A Stylish Obsession," *A&E Biography,* 1996.

Page 45   "We were using . . ." Glenn Plaskin, "Calvin Klein: Playboy Interview," *Playboy,* May 1984.

Page 45   "The only way . . ." Ibid.

Chapter 4

Page 46   "Why don't you . . ." Janice Dickinson, *No Lifeguard on Duty,* HarperCollins, 2002. The quoted price for an additional interview with Dickinson for this book was $3,000, which was declined.

Page 46   "A designer who designs . . ." Ralph Di Gennaro, "Men's Style; The New Appeal of Designer Underwear," *New York Times,* September 12, 1982.

Page 46   "The look the model . . ." National Cotton Council of America.

Page 47   "Not only did this . . ." *New York Times,* August 29, 1982.

Page 47   "In the first five days . . ." Ralph Di Gennaro, "Men's Style, The New Appeal of Designer Underwear," *New York Times,* September 12, 1982.

Page 48   "I wouldn't have done underwear . . ." Ibid.

Page 48   "The posters incite . . ." Glenn Plaskin, "Calvin Klein: Playboy Interview," *Playboy,* May 1984.

Page 48   "That it's selling . . ." Ralph Di Gennaro, "Men's Style; The New Appeal of Designer Underwear," *New York Times,* September 12, 1982.

Page 49   "Men's briefs are . . ." Glenn Plaskin, "Calvin Klein: Playboy Interview," *Playboy,* May 1984.

Page 49   "The company originally projected . . ." Ibid.

Page 49   "However, after 200 stores . . ." Steven Gaines and Sharon Churcher, *Obsession: The Lives and Times of Calvin Klein,* Birch Lane Press, 1994.

Page 50   "In August 1984 . . ." Michael Gross, "The Latest Calvin," *New York* magazine, August 8, 1988.

Page 50 "And in a twist . . ." "Wickes buying G&W in a $1.1 Billion Deal," *New York Times News Service,* June 11, 1985.

Page 51 "I've never seen . . ." *Back to the Future* script, Robert Zemeckis and Bob Gale, 1985.

Chapter 5

Page 52 "In 1982, jeans licensee . . ." *Dow Jones News Service,* January 20, 1983.

Page 54 "We disagreed about . . ." Glenn Plaskin, "Calvin Klein: Playboy Interview," *Playboy,* May 1984.

Page 54 "Andrew would be . . ." *Wall Street Journal,* September 6, 1983.

Page 54 "Klein and Schwartz didn't sit . . ." Steven Gaines and Sharon Churcher, *Obsession: The Lives and Times of Calvin Klein,* Birch Lane Press, 1994.

Page 54 "Blaming 'unexpectedly slow . . .' " "Puritan Fashion Says 1983 Net Won't Match Prior Estimate," *Dow Jones News Service,* October 6, 1983.

Page 55 "Profits were sliding . . ." Glenn Plaskin, "Calvin Klein: Playboy Interview," *Playboy,* May 1984.

Page 55 "Andrew is a nice . . ." Ibid.

Page 55 "On November 14, 1983 . . ." "Calvin Klein Offers to Buy Puritan Fashion Corp.," *Dow Jones News Service,* November 14, 1983.

Page 55 "We don't anticipate . . ." Ibid.

Page 55 "And if the board . . ." "Calvin Klein Threatens Hostile Bid for Puritan," *Dow Jones News Service,* November 25, 1983.

Page 56 "We have concluded . . ." Ibid.

Page 56 "Further, Klein said . . ." Ibid.

Page 56 "The decision came down . . ." "Calvin Klein Offers to Buy Puritan Fashion Corp.," *Dow Jones News Service,* November 14, 1983.

Page 56 "There was some . . ." "Puritan Fashions Accepts Offer from Calvin Klein," *Dow Jones News Service,* November 29, 1983.

Chapter 6

Page 57 "I'm good-looking . . ." Author's interview.

Page 57 "The biggest thing . . ." Author's interview, informed source.

Page 58 "Steve Rubell was . . ." Ibid.

Page 58 "The development of . . ." Multiple sources.

Page 59   "In the history of . . ." Author's interview.

Page 60   "I bought every . . ." Michael Gross, "The Latest Calvin," *New York* magazine, August 8, 1988.

Page 61   "Calvin couldn't break . . ." Ibid.

Page 61   "A week later . . ." Ibid.

Page 61   "We were making . . ." Lisa Lockwood, "Bye Bye Barry," *WWD,* February 13, 2003.

Page 62   "It didn't work . . ." Susan Irvine, "Calvin Clean," *Ottawa Citizen,* March 25, 2000.

Page 62   "Negotiations started . . ." Steven Gaines and Sharon Churcher, *Obsession: The Lives and Times of Calvin Klein,* Birch Lane Press, 1994.

Page 63   "I don't give . . ." Ibid.

Page 64   "Klein agreed to pay . . ." Michael Gross, "The Model Muddle: Up in Arms Over the Object of Calvin Klein's Obsession," *Washington Post,* July 28, 1985.

Page 66   "A firm named . . ." Steven Gaines and Sharon Churcher, *Obsession: The Lives and Times of Calvin Klein,* Birch Lane Press, 1994.

Page 66   "The fragrance is not . . ." Tracy Brobston, "Calvin Klein: You Can't Be Great All the Time," *Dallas Morning News,* May 22, 1985.

Page 66   "The golden liquid was . . ." Genevieve Buck, "Calvin Klein: Nothin' 'Tween him 'n' His Ads," *Chicago Tribune,* May 8, 1985.

Page 66   "I collect tortoiseshell . . ." Tracy Brobston, "Calvin Klein: You Can't Be Great All the Time," *Dallas Morning News,* May 22, 1985.

Page 67   "Once the name evolved . . ." Susan Irvine, "Calvin Clean," *Ottawa Citizen,* March 25, 2000.

Page 67   "Klein said he was 'obsessed . . .' " "Calvin Klein: A Stylish Obsession," *A&E Biography,* 1996.

Page 67   "When one makes . . ." Ruthe Stein, "Selling the Smell of Sex," *San Francisco Chronicle,* March 22, 1985.

Page 67   "She loved me . . ." Elizabeth Kastor, "Ah, the Obsession with It All," *Washington Post,* March 14, 1985.

Page 68   "We were in a warm . . ." Ibid.

Page 68   "My work is . . ." Genevieve Buck, "Calvin Klein: Nothin' 'Tween him 'n' His Ads," *Chicago Tribune,* May 8, 1985.

Page 68   "This is my first . . ." Tracy Brobston, "Calvin Klein: You Can't Be Great All the Time," *Dallas Morning News,* May 22, 1985.

Page 69 "We're now making . . ." Genevieve Buck, "Obsession for Ad Erotica," *The Record,* January 23, 1986.

Page 69 "Appropriately, *Time* magazine . . ." Janice Castro, "Calvin Meets the Marlboro Man," *Time,* October 21, 1985.

Chapter 7

Page 70 "Kelly Rector came from . . ." Steven Gaines and Sharon Churcher, *Obsession: The Lives and Times of Calvin Klein,* Birch Lane Press, 1994.

Page 70 "The second I sat . . ." Beth Whitehouse, "A New Book, a New Life," *Newsday,* October 5, 2000.

Page 70 "Even as a child, Kelly . . ." Nina Hyde, "Calvin Klein Marries," *Washington Post,* September 27, 1986.

Page 71 "I got a call . . ." Author's interview.

Page 72 "Around the office, Rector . . ." Michael Gross, "The Latest Calvin," *New York* magazine, August 8, 1988.

Page 73 "He was the fantasy of Calvin's gut . . ." Author's interview, informed source.

Page 73 "Instead of Klein . . ." Nina Hyde, "Calvin's Disappearing Act," *Washington Post,* May 6, 1984.

Page 74 "Days later, Carr left . . ." Timothy Hawkins, "Carr Is in Driver's Seat with New Label," *Los Angeles Times,* March 21, 1986.

Page 74 "When she spent . . ." Michael Gross, "The Latest Calvin," *New York* magazine, August 8, 1988.

Page 74 "Rector, by design . . ." Nina Hyde, "Fashion Notes," *Washington Post,* September 21, 1986.

Page 74 "On this trip . . ." "Calvin Klein Takes a Designer Bride," *United Press International,* September 27, 1986.

Page 74 "Klein later put . . ." Beth Whitehouse, "A New Book, a New Life," *Newsday,* October 5, 2000.

Page 75 "The designer paid . . ." Susan Mulcahy, "Kelly's Partner a Gem of a Guy," *Newsday,* April 13, 1986.

Page 76 "I did buy Kelly . . ." Melissa Sones, "On the Brink of Eternity," *Newsday,* May 11, 1988.

Page 77 "And Schwartz considers the name . . ." Lisa Lockwood, "Bye Bye Barry," *WWD,* February, 13, 2003.

Page 77 "Burns devised a strategy . . ." Robin Wiest, "From Here to Eternity," *WWD,* May 19, 1988.

Page 77 "I think you can look . . ." Susan Irvine, "Calvin Clean," *Ottawa Citizen,* March 25, 2000.

Page 78 "A little less than two weeks ago . . ." *United Press International,* "Being Treated in Drug-Alcohol Clinic," *Los Angeles
Times,* May 9, 1988.

Page 78 "I'm in the first year . . ." Maureen Orth, "A Shaky Calvin Klein
Puts His Life Back Together," *Toronto Star,* October 9, 1988.

Page 78 "I hope it does . . ." Melissa Sones, "On the Brink of Eternity,"
Newsday, May 11, 1988.

Page 79 "I'm thinking I'm . . ." Ibid.

Page 79 "Would you still love me . . ." James Cox, "New TV Ads Capture Attention for Eternity," *USA Today,* September 14, 1988.

Page 79 "What happened is that . . ." Author's interview, informed
source.

Page 80 "Zack and Kelly became . . ." George Carr, *Zack Carr,* power-
House Books, 2002.

Chapter 8

Page 82 "Required filings with the . . ." Joan Kron and Donald Moffitt,
"Calvin Klein Borrows $70 Million at High Rates to Pay Debt,"
Wall Street Journal, October 9, 1985.

Page 82 "The pressures of meeting . . ." Ibid.

Page 82 "For instance, SEC . . ." Ibid.

Page 84 "Klein and Schwartz paid dearly . . ." Steven Gaines and
Sharon Churcher, *Obsession: The Lives and Times of Calvin
Klein,* Birch Lane Press, 1994.

Page 84 "We bought back . . ." Michael Gross, "Bad Week for Calvin,"
New York Times, June 16, 1987.

Page 85 "By March 1986 . . ." "Investors Acquire 6.7% Stake in Minnetonka's Common Shares," *Dow Jones News Service,* March
31, 1986.

Page 85 "Meanwhile, Minnetonka was . . ." Susan E. Peterson,
"Steinem Shows That Feminism Can Live with an Obsession"
Star-Tribune (Twin Cities), July 25, 1987.

Page 85 "The duo continued . . ." "Calvin Klein Indus Founders Boost
Minnetonka Stock to 9.2%," *Dow Jones News Service,* August
17, 1987. And "Calvin Klein Unit Boosts Minnetonka Stake to
12.7%," *Dow Jones News Service,* December 23, 1987.

Page 85 "However, Klein and Schwartz . . ." Jim Jones, "Minnetonka
Inc. 'doesn't fear' Klein takeover," *Star-Tribune* (Twin Cities),
December 24, 1987.

Page 85 "In what was seen as . . ." Mona Lerner, "Minnetonka Corp.

Downplays Talk of Takeover by Calvin Klein," *Star-Tribune* (Twin Cities), January 8, 1987.

Page 86 "In early 1989, he . . ." "Unilever and Minnetonka Reach Merger Agreement," *PR Newswire,* July 2, 1989.

Page 86 "Klein and Schwartz emerged . . ." Francine Schuadel, "Minnetonka Corp. Agrees to Be Sold to Unilever Unit," *Star-Tribune* (Twin Cities), July 3, 1989.

Page 86 "The company reported a loss . . ." Teri Agins and Jeffrey A. Trachtenberg, "Designer Troubles," *Wall Street Journal,* November 22, 1991.

Page 87 "In 1991, the company . . ." Steve Farnsworth, "Ad Cuts Help Calvin Klein Profits Rise," *WWD,* November 15, 1991.

Page 88 "David went into the market . . ." "Calvin Klein: A Stylish Obsession," *A&E Biography,* 1996.

Page 88 "I believe Calvin . . ." Lisa Lockwood, "Calvin Klein: A New Deal Brings Relief," *WWD,* May 7, 1992.

Chapter 9

Page 89 "He understands the zeitgeist . . ." Author's interview, informed source.

Page 90 "You could see . . ." Author's interview.

Page 91 "We had a ritual . . ." Ibid.

Page 91 "He later became . . ." Ibid.

Page 91 "Calvin and Barry bought . . ." Ibid.

Page 92 "When Donna Karen diffused . . ." Ibid.

Page 93 "My proposal was . . ." Ibid.

Page 93 "The negotiations with . . ." Author's interview, informed source.

Page 93 "Calvin sees the . . ." Ibid.

Page 95 "It cost the company . . ." "Calvin Klein Raises Brows Thigh High with Latest Advertisement through Vanity Fair," *Marketing Week,* October 4, 1991.

Page 95 "He wanted to . . ." Ibid.

Page 95 "Klein supported the piece . . ." "Calvin Jump-Starts His Jeans," *WWD,* September 12, 1991.

Page 95 "Bloomingdale's reported that . . ." Constance C. R. White, "Calvin Klein: Jeans Provocateur," *WWD,* November 6, 1991.

Page 95 "I always try to make . . ." Ibid.

Page 96 "Federated Department Stores . . ." Teri Agins, "Klein Jeans' Sexy Insert Didn't Spur Sales," *Wall Street Journal,* May 5, 1992.

Page 96 "That was the old . . ." Author's interview.

Page 96 "Calvin's extremely innovative . . ." Author's interview, informed source.

Page 98 "I actually ran into . . ." Author's interview.

Page 98 "I'm not into . . ." Lisa Lockwood, "Calvin Finds a Real Woman," *WWD,* February 7, 1992.

Page 101 "Marky's involvement was . . ." "Calvin Klein Announces the Launch of a Multi-Million-Dollar Campaign Featuring Marky Mark," *Business Wire,* September 29, 1992.

Page 102 "The first place we debuted . . ." Author's interview, informed source.

Page 102 "Shouts go out . . ." Lisa Lockwood, "Red-Hot Marky Puts His Rap on Calvin Briefs," *WWD,* October 20, 1992.

Page 102 "One night . . ." "Calvin Klein: A Stylish Obsession," *A&E Biography,* 1996.

Page 103 "The initial idea . . ." Author's interview, informed source.

Page 104 "The Nineties are about . . ." Iain R. Webb, "Dress to Obsess," *Times* (London), March 12, 1994.

Page 104 "The newest cK . . ." Genevieve Buck, "The New Calvin Rejuvenated by His Return to Menswear and a Strong Creative Surge," *Chicago Tribune,* September 30, 1992.

Page 105 "Marky Mark was truly . . ." Author's interview, informed source.

Chapter 10

Page 106 "Using the company's licensing income . . ." Sidney Rutberg and Lisa Lockwood, "Calvin Buys Out Geffen," *WWD,* June 17, 1993.

Page 106 "He's one of the smartest . . ." Ibid.

Page 107 "For these potentially valuable . . ." Karyn Monget, "Underwear's Power Pair," *WWD,* February 6, 1995.

Page 108 "For Warnaco, this acquisition . . ." Ibid.

Page 108 "Simon's company, Rio Sportswear . . ." Maryellen Gordon, "Calvin in Pact to Sell cK Jeans to Rio for $35 Million," *WWD,* February 11, 1994.

Page 108 "Jeans started as a license . . ." Ibid.

Page 109 "I didn't like . . ." Janet Ozzard, "Simon: Big Names, Big Plans," *WWD,* November 21, 1996.

Page 109 "By April 1994 . . ." Teri Agins, "Fruit of the Loom Said Likely to Buy Calvin Klein Jeans," *Wall Street Journal,* April 20, 1994.

Page 109 "I had a feeling . . ." Janet Ozzard, "Simon: Big Names, Big Plans," *WWD*, November 21, 1996.

Page 110 "Calvin was leading . . ." Author's interview, informed source.

Page 110 "You have this gorgeous girl . . ." Ibid.

Page 111 "She wasn't telling people . . ." Ibid.

Page 111 "With collection and cK . . ." Ibid.

Page 111 "Klein even 'sent out a memo . . .' " Ibid.

Page 112 "One source suggested . . ." Ibid.

Page 114 "Calvin is on a roll . . ." Teri Agins, "Calvin Klein Names Forte, Executive at Rival Armani, to Two Key Positions," *Wall Street Journal*, May 24, 1994.

Page 115 "Barry and I will be . . ." Lisa Lockwood, "Klein Sees Forte as Key to Global Growth Plans," *WWD*, May 24, 1994.

Page 115 "The office never . . ." Author's interview, informed source.

Page 115 "We were constantly using . . ." Ibid.

Page 116 "The next day . . ." Author's interview, multiple sources.

Page 116 "Before her arrival . . ." Author's interview.

Page 116 "Before, 'everybody reported to both . . .' " Author's interview, informed source.

Page 117 "The Saks contingent included . . ." Ibid.

Page 117 "You tell that woman . . ." Ibid.

Page 119 "Susan Sokol had . . ." Ibid.

Page 120 "Expectations were lofty . . ." Koji Hirano, "Klein Sees Japan Volume Above $3 B Over 10 Years," *WWD*, March 18, 1994.

Page 121 "The Stefanel business," Author's interview, informed source.

Page 121 "The vibrant core . . ." Jonathan Auerbach, "Calvin Klein Moves into Home Products Business," *New York Post*, June 3, 1994.

Chapter 11

Page 123 "Forget about the . . ." Author's interview.

Page 123 "The resulting fragrance . . ." Calvin Klein Cosmetics company release, June 24, 1994.

Page 123 "The goal on . . ." Author's interview, informed source.

Page 124 "They had to go . . ." Ibid.

Page 124 "No one had done . . ." Ibid.

Page 124 "I know it's . . ." Author's interview.

Page 124 "Sales expectations for . . ." Julie Belcove, "cK one Dominates Fragrance Launches, Shatters Projections," *WWD*, October 7, 1994.

Page 125 "A frenzy ensued . . ." Author's interview, informed source.

Page 125 "Normally when things are . . ." Ibid.

Page 125 "It was the thing . . ." Ibid.

Page 125 "And though the campaign . . ." Soren Larson, "cK one Campaign: The Genderless Scent Will Have Sexless Ads," *WWD,* August 5, 1994.

Page 126 "Because the license . . ." Author's interview, informed source.

Page 126 "What everybody agreed . . ." Author's interview.

Page 127 "Those were the ads . . ." Author's interview, informed source.

Page 127 "She's been known . . ." Ibid.

Page 127 "The off-camera voice originally . . ." Page Six, "Calvin Ads Dropped Porn Host," *New York Post,* September 14, 1995.

Page 128 "Are you strong . . ." Bob Garfield, "Publicity Monster Turns on Klein," *Ad Age,* September 4, 1995.

Page 128 "The print ads . . ." Kevin Goldman, "Calvin Klein Ad Rekindles Debate as It Runs in Youths' Magazine," *Wall Street Journal,* July 10, 1995.

Page 128 "A spokesman for . . ." Ibid.

Page 129 "Some people have . . ." Statement from Calvin Klein, Inc., August 10, 1995.

Page 129 "We are stunned . . ." Statement from Calvin Klein, Inc., August 21, 1995.

Page 129 "All kinds of people . . ." Author's interview.

Page 130 "After the press conference . . ." Ibid.

Page 130 "Calvin Klein ran . . ." Statement from Calvin Klein, Inc., August 28, 1995.

Page 130 "We were told . . ." Author's interview, informed source.

Page 131 "The floor needs . . ." Ibid.

Page 132 "The downtown store . . ." Ibid.

Page 132 "I got the assignment . . ." Author's interview.

Page 133 "The American Family Association was fueling . . ." Statement from the American Family Association, August 29, 1995.

Page 134 "We're very confident . . ." Paula Span, "Sexy Calvin Klein Ads Spark FBI Inquiry," *Washington Post,* September 8, 1995.

Page 134 "I don't have any . . ." "Clinton raps cK ads," *Ad Age,* September 22, 1995.

Page 134 "We did a fragrance ad . . ." Michele Ingrassia, "Calvin's World," *Newsweek,* September 11, 1995.

Page 135 "This ad . . ." Karyn Monget, Lisa Lockwood, "Warnaco's Wachner Stands by Calvin—but not by that ad," *WWD,* November 3, 1995.

Page 135 "To me that was . . ." Author's interview, informed source.

Page 135 "Once again a 'shared' fragrance . . ." *European Cosmetics Markets,* August 1, 1996.

Page 136 "Sales were expected . . ." Pete Born, "cK be: Chartbuster's Sequel," *WWD,* May 24, 1996.

Page 136 "It is 'a close up look . . .' " "Calvin Klein Cosmetics Launches Advertising Campaign for New Fragrance cK be," Calvin Klein Cosmetics press release, August 14, 1996.

Page 136 "One 'model' . . ." Page Six, "Heroin Chic," *New York Post,* August 21, 1996.

Page 136 "I've squatted . . ." Ibid.

Page 136 "Be a saint. Be . . ." Mimi Avins, "By Design by Letting People Be, Klein's Ads Break 'Rules,' " *Los Angeles Times,* December 5, 1996.

Page 137 "The glorification . . ." "Calvin Klein: A Stylish Obsession," *A&E Biography,* 1996.

Page 138 "We are still . . ." Liz Smith, "Something Comes Between Her & Her Calvin: A Split," *New York Post,* August 13, 1996.

Page 138 "They were very . . ." Author's interview, informed source.

Page 138 "In fact, in both . . ." Multiple sources.

Chapter 12

Page 139 "Simon, a burly . . ." Wendy Bounds, "Are Calvin Klein and Wachner Too Tight to Get Along," *Wall Street Journal,* September 26, 1997.

Page 139 "Annual sales . . ." Carol Emert, "Calvin Klein's Jeans Licensee Files for IPO," *WWD,* March 13, 1996.

Page 140 "The company hoped . . ." "Designer Holdings IPO: In Talks to Boost Revolver," Select Federal Filings Newswires, March 14, 1996.

Page 140 "It did come . . ." "Cashing in," *WWD,* March 14, 1996.

Page 140 "The market is buying . . ." Brian Milner, "Fashion Firms Dazzle the Drab Wall Street Crowd," *Globe and Mail,* May 21, 1996.

Page 140 "The enthusiastic anticipation . . ." "Designer Holdings IPO Gets $18 Tag," *WWD,* May 10, 1996.

Page 141 "And on its . . ." "Excel, Other IPOs Soar in Buoyant Market," *Reuters News,* May 10, 1996.

Page 141 "The deal sewed up . . ." "Holding On," *WWD,* May 23, 1996.

Page 141 "The company filed . . ." "CK vs. Conway" *WWD,* September 26, 1996.

Page 142 "Nine traffickers were . . ." Designer Holdings company statement, June 24, 1997.

Page 142 "After its stunning debut . . ." "Wall Street Hits Designer Holdings' Cut Back Plan," *Daily News Record,* March 21, 1997.

Page 142 "However, he warned . . ." Designer Holdings company statement, March 19, 1997.

Page 142 "In the age . . ." "Designer Holdings Cuts Outlook for Sales in '97," *WWD,* March 20, 1997.

Page 142 "It hit a low . . ." "Wall Street Hits Designer Holdings' Cutback Plan," *Daily News Record,* March 21, 1997.

Page 143 "While the company . . ." "Designer Holdings Buyback," *Wall Street Journal,* August 22, 1997.

Page 143 "We know how to create . . ." Laura Bird and Wendy Bounds, "Warnaco to Acquire Designer Holdings with Shares Valued at $354 Million," *Wall Street Journal,* September 18, 1997.

Page 143 "She had negotiated . . ." Laura Bird and Wendy Bounds, "Warnaco Group Is in Talks to Acquire Designer Holdings," *Wall Street Journal,* September 16, 1997.

Page 143 "Wachner's offer . . ." Warnaco/Designer Holdings company statement, September 25, 1997.

Page 143 "Warnaco's Calvin Klein underwear . . ." Karyn Monget and Sidney Rutberg, "Wachner's New Deal: Warnaco Bids $345 M for Calvin's Jeans," *WWD,* September 18, 1997.

Page 144 "They were reassured . . ." Thomas J. Ryan, "With Quips and Kisses, Wachner Takes Over cK Jeans Business," *WWD,* December 15, 1997.

Page 144 "Obviously, Linda and . . ." Karyn Monget, "Warnaco, DH Seal the Deal," *WWD,* September 26, 1997.

Page 144 "There were regular . . ." Multiple sources. Wachner's dog, EBITDA, was named after the common accounting acronym for "earnings before interest, taxes, depreciation, and amortization."

Page 144 "I remember meeting . . ." Author's interview, informed source.

Page 146 "I know with the creative . . ." Ibid.

Page 146 "In professional advertising . . ." Author's interview.

Page 147 "Showing the advertisement . . ." Chelsea J. Carter, "Calvin Klein's Children's Underwear Ad Pulled," *Associated Press,* February 18, 1999.

Page 147 "The decision [to pull . . ." Author's interview, informed source.

Page 147 "The advertising campaign . . ." Calvin Klein company statement, February 17, 1999.

Page 148 "You know the old saying . . ." Author's interview.

Page 148 "You see other . . ." Tracy Connor, "Kid-Ad Furor Is No Sales Boon: Calvin," *New York Post,* February 20, 1999.

Page 149 "The designer had . . ." Teri Agins, *The End of Fashion,* William Morrow & Co., 1999.

Chapter 13

Page 150 "By the late . . ." Tom Ryan, "Next IPO from Calvin?" *WWD,* June 18, 1997.

Page 151 "I'm not leaving . . ." Edward Nardoza and Sharon Edelson, "Forte to Relinquish Key Calvin Klein Posts, but Remain as Advisor," *WWD,* June 9, 1999.

Page 151 "Instead, her office . . ." Author's interview, informed source.

Page 152 "In October 1999, . . ." Calvin Klein company announcement, October 6, 1999.

Page 152 "Calvin Klein, Inc., was . . ." Ibid.

Page 153 "LVMH's Bernard Arnault . . ." Evelyn Nussenbaum, "Klein Wants to Shed His Calvins—Fashion King Puts Empire Up for Sale," *New York Post,* October 7, 1999.

Page 153 "Fueled with $1.62 billion . . ." "Calvin Puts Himself in Play," *WWD,* October 6, 1999.

Page 153 "As an aside, Tom Ford . . ." Sara Gay Forden, *The House of Gucci: A Sensational Story of Murder, Madness, Glamour and Greed,* William Morrow, 2000.

Page 155 "We're not in the bidding . . ." Evelyn Nussenbaum, "Wachner Nixes Bid for Calvin; Warnaco Content as Licensee," *New York Post,* December 29, 1999.

Page 155 ". . . offered only $600 million." Patricia Sellers, "Seventh Avenue Smackdown," *Fortune,* September 4, 2000.

Page 155 "I think the best . . ." Evelyn Nussenbaum, "Wachner Nixes Bid for Calvin; Warnaco Content as Licensee," *New York Post,* December 29, 1999.

Page 155 "While it was still . . ." Author's interview.

Page 155 "We have been invited . . ." "Italy's HdP Studying Bid for Calvin Klein," *Reuters News,* January 11, 2000.

Page 155 "The problem with . . ." Evelyn Nussenbaum, "Aspiring Fashion Titan Owner of Valentino and Fila Eyes a Bid for Calvin Klein," *New York Post,* February 6, 2000.

Page 156 "We are no longer . . ." Evelyn Nussenbaum, "HdP Drops Out of Calvin Klein Bidding," *New York Post,* March 8, 2000.

Page 156 "My company reached . . ." Author's interview.

Page 157 "One alternative that kept . . ." Ibid.

Page 157 "We were convinced . . ." Ibid.

Page 157   "It was difficult . . ." Ibid.

Page 158   "When we matched, . . ." Calvin Klein company statement, April 18, 2000.

Page 158   "The buyer 'would . . .' " Sonia Purnell, "Calvin Klein Goes Out of Fashion," *Independent on Sunday,* February 27, 2000.

Page 158   "I don't think . . ." Lisa Lockwood, "Bye Bye Barry," *WWD,* February 13, 2003.

Chapter 14

Page 159   "On May 30, 2000 . . ." Calvin Klein Trademark Trust and Calvin Klein, Inc., against Linda Wachner, Warnaco Group, Inc., Warnaco Inc., Designer Holdings, Ltd., CKJ Holdings, Inc., Jeanswear Holdings Inc., Calvin Klein Jeanswear Co., and Outlet Holdings, Inc., filed May 30, 2000.

Page 159   "They even took . . ." Patricia Sellers, "Seventh Avenue Smackdown," *Fortune,* September 4, 2000.

Page 160   "Wachner's first inkling . . ." Ibid.

Page 160   "Warnaco and Wachner herself . . ." Calvin Klein Trademark Trust and Calvin Klein, Inc., against Linda Wachner, Warnaco Group, Inc., Warnaco Inc., Designer Holdings, Ltd., CKJ Holdings, Inc., Jeanswear Holdings Inc., Calvin Klein Jeanswear Co., and Outlet Holdings, Inc., filed May 30, 2000.

Page 160   "Topping the list . . ." Calvin Klein company release, May 31, 2000.

Page 161   "The JC Penny issue . . ." Calvin Klein Trademark Trust and Calvin Klein, Inc., against Linda Wachner, Warnaco Group, Inc., Warnaco Inc., Designer Holdings, Ltd., CKJ Holdings, Inc., Jeanswear Holdings Inc., Calvin Klein Jeanswear Co., and Outlet Holdings, Inc., filed May 30, 2000.

Page 161   "In addition, Warnaco made . . ." Ibid.

Page 161   "Warnaco breached its . . ." Ibid.

Page 161   "Over the past 30 years . . ." Ibid.

Page 162   "Having tried and failed . . ." Evelyn Nussenbaum, "Wachner Rips Calvin—Questions Motives Behind Surprise Suit," *New York Post,* June 1, 2000.

Page 162   "In preparation for the . . ." Author's interview, informed source.

Page 162   "This is a difficult . . ." Evelyn Nussenbaum, "Fashion Titan's Fight: Disappointed Designer Vows to Regain Rights to His Brand," *New York Post,* June 4, 2000.

Page 162   "He also charged . . ." Lisa Lockwood, Vicki M. Young and

Janet Ozzard, "Calvin and His Warnaco Suit Steal the Scene at CEO Summit," *WWD,* June 2, 2000.

Page 163 "Repeatedly over the past . . ." *Larry King Live,* CNN, June 5, 2000.

Page 163 "Every time he . . ." Lisa Lockwood and Vicki M. Young, "Should Linda Work the Media?" *WWD,* June 9, 2000.

Page 164 "The complaint is . . ." Warnaco company statement, June 5, 2000.

Page 164 "Wachner hired equally . . ." Vicki M. Young, "Date Set for Calvin/Warnaco Trial," *WWD,* June 21, 2000.

Page 164 "Wachner, who herself was . . ." Author's interview, informed source.

Page 164 "CKI has abdicated . . ." Calvin Klein Trademark Trust and Calvin Klein, Inc., plaintiffs v. Warnaco Group, Inc., Warnaco Inc., Designer Holdings, Ltd., CKJ Holdings, Inc., Jeanswear Holdings, Inc., Calvin Klein Jeanswear Co., and Outlet Holdings, Inc., defendant-counterclaimants, and Linda Wachner, defendant, v. Calvin Klein and Calvin Klein, Inc., counter-claim-defendants, filed June 26, 2000.

Page 165 "The countersuit charged . . ." Ibid.

Page 165 "In July 2000 . . ." Paul Tharp, "Warnaco Hammered After Profit Warning," *New York Post,* July 21, 2000.

Page 166 "In early August . . ." Vicki M. Young, "Court Lets Wachner out of 4 Counts in Klein Suit," *WWD,* August 7, 2000.

Page 166 "What we have here . . ." Ibid.

Page 166 "In October, the court . . ." Vicki M. Young, "A Win for Wachner," *WWD,* October 11, 2000.

Page 166 "The licensing agreement . . ." Author's own reporting, "Calvin's New Beef: Warnaco Has Too Much Debt," *New York Post,* January 10, 2001.

Page 167 "By 9 A.M. . . ." Author's own reporting.

Page 167 "My law clerks . . ." Ibid.

Page 167 "At this point . . ." Ibid.

Page 167 "The parties believe . . ." Calvin Klein, Inc., and Warnaco press release, January 22, 2001.

Page 168 "The straw that broke . . ." Author's interview, informed source.

Chapter 15

Page 169 "Klein's big Asian . . ." Miles Socha, Lisa Lockwood, Koji Hirano, "Mulling Bids for Firm, Calvin Takes Charge of His Brand in Japan," *WWD,* January 4, 2000.

Page 169 "The enormous Stefanel . . ." Samantha Conti, "Calvin Klein, Stefanel End Bridge Agreement for Europe, Mideast," *WWD*, March 1, 2001.

Page 170 "The company's license . . ." Eric Wilson and Samantha Conti, "Calvin Taking Action, Buys Back Signature License from Burani," *WWD*, June 29, 2001.

Page 170 "To one former insider, . . ." Author's interview, informed source.

Page 170 "Over the next . . ." www.punto.com, March 23, 2001.

Page 170 "Later that spring . . ." Calvin Klein company release, May 8, 2001.

Page 170 "If you look . . ." Eric Wilson and Lisa Lockwood, "Calvin Cleans House: Dozens Are Laid Off, cK Shut Down in US," *WWD*, May 9, 2001.

Page 171 "The collection . . ." Author's own reporting, "Calvin's Big Plans—Slates Retail Expansion Overseas," *New York Post*, May 10, 2001.

Page 171 "We want to open . . ." Ibid.

Page 172 "I don't feel this . . ." Eric Wilson, "Calvin Klein: After 33 Years in Business, The Designer Remains True to His Quest for Modernity While Searching for What's Next," *WWD*, June 5, 2001.

Page 172 "It is as . . ." Author's own reporting.

Page 173 "With more than . . ." Author's own reporting, "Warnaco Bankrupt: Wachner OK'd on $600 M in Financing," *New York Post*, June 12, 2001.

Page 173 "On June 11 . . ." Ibid.

Page 174 "The decision . . ." Patricia Sellers, "Linda Wachner Is Out—Well, Sort Of," *Fortune*, December 10, 2001.

Page 174 "When you're in . . ." Author's own reporting, "Wachner Busted! Warnaco CEO Fired," *New York Post*, November 17, 2001.

Chapter 16

Page 177 "I met Bruce . . ." Lisa Lockwood, "Bye Bye Barry," *WWD*, February 13, 2003.

Page 177 "Polish immigrant Moses Phillips . . ." "Phillips-Van Heusen Corporation," *Hoovers Company Profiles*, April 10, 2003.

Page 177 "The Van Heusen label . . ." Bernice Kanner, "Van Heusen Brings Back Wrinkle-Free Reagan," *New York Daily News*, January 13, 1981.

Page 177 "The company was . . ." Paul Tharp, "Van Heusen Corp. Collars a New Chief," *New York Post,* May 2, 1993.

Page 178 "While PVH . . ." Calvin Klein company press release, August 21, 2002.

Page 178 "PVH partnered with . . ." Erica Copulsky, Lisa Marsh, "Kelly's Pal Wins Plum Banking Role," *New York Post,* November 18, 2002.

Page 178 "The duo first . . ." Sidney Rutberg, "Citibank, Which Captured the Attention of Seventh Avenue with Two . . ." *WWD,* July 12, 1993.

Page 178 "In 1990 . . ." June Fletcher, "Private Properties," *Wall Street Journal,* June 2, 2000.

Page 179 "We would be willing . . ." Phillips-Van Heusen conference call, November 21, 2002.

Page 179 "We are continuing . . ." Eric Wilson, "Calvin and Warnaco Back to Square One," *WWD,* December 12, 2002.

Page 180 "Klein had waited . . ." Author's own reporting, "Calvin Klein has a Payday Obsession," *New York Post,* November 24, 2002.

Page 180 "On the morning . . ." Phillips-Van Heusen company press release, December 17, 2002.

Page 180 "At the close of . . ." Phillips-Van Heusen company press release, December 17, 2002.

Page 180 "This is without . . ." Phillips-Van Heusen conference call, December 17, 2002.

Page 181 "We've already begun . . ." Ibid.

Page 181 "Barry and I have . . ." Author's own reporting.

Page 181 "We were in total . . ." Lisa Lockwood, "Bye Bye Barry," *WWD,* February 13, 2003.

Chapter 17

Page 184 "Phillips-Van Heusen has lofty . . ." Phillips-Van Heusen company press release, December 17, 2003.

Page 184 "As with most of the other . . ." Ibid.

Page 184 "It is interesting to note . . ." "Calvin Klein Reaches Agreement in Principle for Strategic Partnership with Vestimenta on Designer Collection Businesses," press release, February 27, 2003.

Page 185 "Unbeknownst to most . . ." *WWD,* February 18, 2003.

Page 185 "The former chairman . . ." John Crittenden, "Noe Resigns as NYRA Head," *Palm Beach Post,* October 12, 2000.

Page 185 "However, the language . . ." Phillips-Van Heusen SEC Form 8-K, filed 17 December, 2002.

Page 186 "I just can't see . . ." Author's interview, informed source.

Page 186 "The deal to sell . . ." Phillips-Van Heusen company press release, December 17, 2003.

Page 187 "Bruce and myself . . ." Phillips-Van Heusen conference call, March 5, 2003.

Page 187 "Designer Jeffrey Banks believes . . ." Author's interview.

Page 187 "We would do . . ." Ibid.

Page 188 "The customer is much smarter . . ." Ibid.

Page 188 "Rumors circulated . . ." "Fashion Scoops," *WWD,* March 5, 2003.

Page 189 "Still, 'I think Narciso . . .'" Author's interview, informed source.

Page 188 "Perhaps Calvin Klein . . ." Michael Gross, "The Latest Calvin," *New York* magazine, August 8, 1988.

Epilogue

Page 190 "Calvin's lower-priced . . ." Author's interview, informed source.

Page 191 "The truth of . . ." Ibid.

Page 191 "In his subconscious . . ." Ibid.

Page 192 "The world was clued . . ." Multiple sources.

Page 192 "For many years . . ." Calvin Klein statement, April 4, 2003.

Page 193 "Klein is said . . ." Author's interview, informed source.

Bibliography

Periodicals and Newspapers

Ad Age

Associated Press

Chicago Tribune

Clothes

Daily News Record

Dallas Morning News

Dow Jones News Service

European Cosmetics Markets

Fortune

Globe and Mail

Independent on Sunday

Los Angeles Times

Marketing Week

Newsweek

New York

New York Observer

New York Post

New York Times

New York Times News Service

Ottawa Citizen

Playboy

Newsday

Record (Hackensack, NJ)

Reuters

San Francisco Chronicle

Star-Tribune (Twin Cities)

Time

Times (London)

Toronto Star

United Press International

USA Today

Wall Street Journal

Washington Post

Women's Wear Daily (*WWD*)

Books

Agins, Teri. *The End of Fashion*. New York: William Morrow, 1999.

Bender, Marylin. *The Beautiful People*. New York: Coward-McCann, 1967.

Blass, Bill, edited by Cathy Horyn. *Bare Blass*. New York: HarperCollins, 2002.

Carr, George. *Zack Carr,* powerHouse Books, 2002.

Coleridge, Nicholas. *The Fashion Conspiracy: The Dazzling Inside Story of the Glamorous World of International High Fashion*. New York: Harper and Row, 1988.

Dickinson, Janice. *No Lifeguard on Duty: The Accidental Life of the World's First Supermodel*. New York: HarperCollins, 2002.

Forden, Sara Gay. *The House of Gucci: A Sensational Story of Murder, Madness, Glamour and Greed*. New York: William Morrow, 2000.

Gaines, Steven, and Sharon Churcher. *Obsession: The Lives and Times of Calvin Klein*. New York: Birch Lane Press, 1994.

Gross, Michael. *Genuine Authentic: The Real Life of Ralph Lauren*. New York: HarperCollins, 2003.

Gross, Michael. *Model: The Ugly Business of Beautiful Women*. New York: William Morrow, 1995.

Film and Television

Back to the Future, Robert Zemeckis and Bob Gale, 1985.

Larry King Live, CNN, June 5, 2000.

"Calvin Klein: A Stylish Obsession," *A&E Biography,* 1996.

To view an extensive collection of Calvin Klein print advertising images, visit the "Unofficial Calvin Klein Ads Archive" at http://pobox.upenn.edu/~davidtoc/calvin.html.

Index